In 1994, after working for 20 years as a stockbroker, Keith Tondeur founded Credit Action, the money education charity. Convinced that everyone needs to learn the biblical principles on handling money God's way, he's written over a dozen books on the subject. Keith is a regular speaker at conferences and churches, and was appointed an Officer of the Order of the British Empire in the Birthday 2010 Honours List for Services to Financial Education. Keith and his wife Sue attend Kings Church in Richmond, Yorkshire.

Steve Pierce works at Stewardship, a charity offering financial support services to churches and Christian charities and dedicated to transforming generosity. Ordained in 1985, Steve served in two Anglican parishes and then as a resources officer in the diocese of Liverpool. He speaks and writes on finding financial freedom from both biblical and practical perspectives and is co-author of <www.givingingrace.org>. Steve is married to Tracey and has four children.

YOUR MONEY AND YOUR LIFE

*Learning how to handle money
God's way*

Keith Tondeur and Steve Pierce

First published in Great Britain in 1996

Society for Promoting Christian Knowledge
36 Causton Street
London SW1P 4ST
www.spckpublishing.co.uk

Reprinted with revisions once
Second edition published 2010

British Library Cataloguing-in-Publication Data
A catalogue record for this book is available from the British Library

ISBN 978–0–281–06238–6

1 3 5 7 9 10 8 6 4 2

Typeset by Graphicraft Ltd, Hong Kong
Printed in Great Britain by Ashford Colour Press

Produced on paper from sustainable forests

From Keith:

*To R. T. Kendall, for showing me
the unconditional love of Jesus*

From Steve:

*To Christ Church Walton Breck, who showed me
what generous living is all about*

Contents

Tables

———◆———

ix

Acknowledgements

———◆•◆•◆———

Over the years a number of people have influenced us greatly, either through their writing or through personal friendship. I, Keith, am indebted to Howard Dayton, Gene Getz, Ronald Sider and John White from across the Atlantic, and R. T. Kendall, Roy McCloughry and Rob Parsons closer to home. Several of the ideas propounded in this book originally came from them.

I, Steve, am grateful to Pete and Pam Taylor, who first taught me both faith and giving. My thinking has been stimulated by Kath Rogers, Mike and Nikki Eastwood and others in Liverpool, and by John Preston and the UK Stewardship network. Richard Talbot, Fiona Mearns, Anthony McKernan, Tony Cunliffe and colleagues at Stewardship have blended work with friendship. Last but not at all least, my thanks go to my wife, Tracey, and my four children, who accepted with love and patience that 'Dad's in London again'!

Preface

When W. C. Fields, a lifetime agnostic, was asked why he was reading a Bible on his deathbed, he's said to have replied, 'I'm looking for a loophole!' The Bible's teaching on wealth and possessions can be challenging. We may all be looking for loopholes by the end of *Your Money and Your Life*! Hopefully, however, you'll have begun to feel – as we do – that what the Bible says about money can be liberating and joyful.

It's undoubtedly true that the subject of money isn't an easy one. Culture dictates that it's rarely a topic of conversation at parties, in part because of the potentially embarrassing issues of lifestyle and values that may be raised. More pertinent, perhaps, is the fact that money is a cause of anxiety for many. Research from AXA estimates that 10 million employees believe that money worries affect their performance at work. Some 1.4 million said they'd taken time off work in the last 12 months as a result of money worries, and 1.2 million spend more than four hours a day feeling anxious.[1] We may be worried about debt or pensions or job security, or simply feel that our financial affairs are no longer under our control.

Jesus spoke so much about money because he knew that how we manage this resource affects our emotional well-being, our human happiness and our spiritual health. Through exploring some key biblical principles and showing how to apply them in immensely practical ways, we hope that this book will give you a greater understanding of God's purposes for you, your money and your life.

A final word: though our focus is on personal financial discipleship, we trust readers will bear in mind the bigger picture. Billions of people in a world saturated with the abundance of

God's creation blessings live in abject poverty. What we read here, *and how we act on it*, must make a difference to the poor in our communities and in the Global South. If it doesn't, then our own journey to financial freedom has barely begun.

> Let me hold lightly the things of this earth,
> Transient treasures, what are they worth?
> Moths can corrupt them; rust can decay,
> All their bright beauty fades in a day.
> Let me hold lightly temporal things –
> I, who am deathless, I who wear wings!
> Let me hold fast, Lord, things of the skies,
> Quicken my vision, open my eyes!
> Show me thy riches, glory and grace,
> Boundless as time is, endless as space,
> Let me hold lightly things that are mine –
> Lord, thou dost give me all that is thine.
>   Martha Snell Nicholson[2]

Website

To help you to get the most out of this book and to explore further some of the issues raised, please visit <www.stewardship.org.uk/ymyl>. At various places in the text we have indicated where we think you would find it particularly useful to do so. This web resource is part of the money education website of Stewardship, the Christian charity dedicated to transforming generosity. Here you will find documents and practical tools mentioned in the book. The website also contains a wide range of other resources addressing issues of money and discipleship.

YOUR MONEY AND YOUR LIFE

1

Heart problem?

Money is a big part of our daily life. Many of us spend hours each day earning it. We buy things, own things and consume things. It's quite easy to start taking what we have for granted – and to want still more.

We may not even be aware of it, but our attitude to money can powerfully influence our outlook on life, and the way we see ourselves. It's partly for this reason that the events of 2008 had such impact. What began as concern over sub-prime mortgage lending in the United States quickly turned into a global economic crisis. It cost many people their jobs and some, tragically, their homes as well. Our confidence in financial institutions was shaken, and millions of us have been left anxious about our levels of borrowing.

How do we live as disciples of Jesus in such circumstances? And how can we be faithful with the material things – whether many or few – that God has entrusted to us?

'All good gifts around us are sent from heaven above . . .'

Paul teaches that God 'richly provides us with everything for our enjoyment' (1 Tim. 6.17), and this surely is the starting point for thinking about money and possessions. Let us be clear: there's nothing wrong in creating wealth or in owning and consuming material things. God created us as flesh and blood beings, and material things are necessary to our survival and flourishing. They help us fill our space in the world and express ourselves. When Steve was widowed some years ago, he went on a spending spree (wherever possible, we'll be offering ourselves as examples in this book). However, this was more than retail therapy: buying stuff was a way of regaining control over a life that was in pieces, a way of asserting his presence in the world and an expression of some kind of security for his children. As a temporary coping mechanism, it helped. Had it become a habit, it would have been a problem.

When money becomes mammon

Jesus' teaching is blunt and to the point. 'No man can serve two masters: for either he will hate the one, and love the other; or else he will hold to the one, and despise the other. Ye cannot serve God and mammon.' (Matt. 6.24, KJV). Our word 'mammon' comes from the Aramaic *māmōn*. The root meaning may be 'that in which we put our trust', but in Jesus' day the word was used simply to mean money. Money isn't evil, but there are moral issues in wealth creation: it can be entered into justly or in an exploitative way. Goods can be traded fairly or unfairly. Society gives meaning to money, and we can be seduced into believing it represents achievement, status, ambition, identity, power.

Money becomes mammon when we lose the reference points of gratitude, restraint, contentment, gift, trust, community, purpose and, most critical of all, generosity. Money becomes mammon when it no longer serves us but demands and absorbs our attention. Why does Paul quite bluntly refer to the greedy desire for money as idolatry (Col. 3.5; Eph. 5.5)? It's because greed allocates ultimate meaning to wealth and possessions, and ultimate meaning is something of which only God is worthy.

Today our golden calves appear in the car park, in the boardroom, in the corner of our living room or on the pages of our celebrity and lifestyle magazines. We may be silently worshipping money and placing it on the altar of our lives almost without knowing it, by convincing ourselves that we're making our families secure, that we're 'doing it for the kids', that our lifestyle isn't excessive or even that affluence is God's purpose for his faithful people.

> 'If anyone does not refrain from the love of money he will be defiled by idolatry and so be judged as if he were one of the heathen.'   (Polycarp, 70–156, Bishop of Smyrna)

The sound of silence

It may surprise you to learn that there are around 2,300 verses in the Bible on wealth and possessions, compared to around 500 on faith and a similar number on prayer. Long before cash machines or internet banking, money was a real issue to those trying to live the life of God. The challenge is just as pressing today, but how many sermons do we hear on the subject of money? The sound of silence is deafening! This may be because Christian leaders are aware of how hot under the collar people can get when money or lifestyle issues are mentioned. They may dare to preach on tithing, but that can leave us with the feeling that God is only really interested in a maximum of 10 per cent of 'our' money when, in fact, he's interested in the entire 100 per cent. His real longing, though, is for generosity of heart.

Heart problem

It's our attitude to money that will help us resist what author Randy Alcorn calls the strong gravitational pull of wealth, and to be generous with what God has given us, regardless of our income. It's our attitude that will determine whether we ultimately view our possessions as our own or as being entrusted to us by God.

It says in 1 Timothy 6.9–10a: 'People who want to get rich fall into temptation and a trap and into many foolish and harmful desires that plunge men into ruin and destruction. For the love of money is a root of all kinds of evil.' The desire for wealth is a heart problem, and we're all at risk. It's very easy to be enticed into 'improving' our lifestyle, and really quite difficult sometimes to recognize when we have 'enough' and to be satisfied with that. In fact one of the seductions of wealth is that we always define a rich person as someone who has more money than us! Consciously or unconsciously, we may believe that these difficult Bible passages about the rich are aimed at Bill Gates or Richard Branson, or that bloke at work. But by global standards we're all rich, and those awkward verses refer just as much to you and me.

The love of money has consequences: 'Some people, eager for money, have wandered from the faith and pierced themselves with many griefs,' writes Paul in 1 Timothy 6.10b. Let's look briefly at these consequences.

A wrong relationship with money harms our relationship with Jesus

The primary consequence of a love of money for Paul is clear: the desire for wealth erodes our faith. When the Crusades were fought in the Middle Ages, many mercenary soldiers were drafted in. But as they were baptized before going to war, each held his sword out of the water to signify that God was not in control of it. Today, as Christians, we can find ourselves handling our money in a similar fashion. We hold our wallets and purses 'out of the water', saying in effect that God can be Lord of our lives but that we'd rather keep control of our money ourselves.

Each decision we make, conscious or unconscious, to put material things before our trust in God impacts the quality of our spiritual life. But the deception of money is that it does not *feel* as though we're resisting the Lordship of Christ. We

6

just want to provide for our families, pay the mortgage, have a well-earned holiday or replace the car. However, when these things become the practical focus of our lives, we're no longer acting as disciples.

A wrong relationship with money harms our personal well-being

In our consumer society, 'having' has increasingly become more important than 'being'. We all have basic needs for food, shelter and clothing, but we have other needs too. Paul wanted Timothy to bring a cloak to keep him warm *and* scrolls so that he could read, write and feed his mind (2 Tim. 4.13). Security, creativity, laughter, friendship and the freedom to make choices: these are real human needs. The sadness is that chasing shallow short-term wants can mean that meeting these needs is denied us.

A wrong relationship with money harms our personal relationships

The pursuit of money interferes with our relationships, as anyone who's ever fought over a contested will or won the lottery can testify! Strongly materialistic people tend to have less intimacy with others. They're more likely to use people to achieve their goals and less inclined to consider their needs. Money is off the agenda for most couples, although it's cited as one of the chief causes of relationship breakdown in perhaps 70 per cent of cases. A right relationship with money is characterized by transparency, trust, honesty and openness.

> '*I know how very hard it is to be rich and still keep the milk of human kindness. Money has a dangerous way of putting scales on one's eyes, a dangerous way of freezing people's hands, eyes, lips and hearts.*'
> (Dom Hélder Câmara, 1909–99,
> Brazilian theologian and bishop)

A wrong relationship with money blinds us to our obligations to the poor

As the parable of the rich man and Lazarus (Luke 16.19–31) teaches us, we have a God-given responsibility to care for the poor. Lazarus is still with us. He sleeps rough in the cities of the world – hungry, ill and in pain. He may not ask directly for help, and no one may ask on his behalf, but a right relationship with money means that we'll be willing to share any wealth entrusted to us to ease his suffering.

> *'Jesus tells us that people who cry because their hearts are broken over the things that break the heart of God are the fulfilled people in this world.'*
>
> *(Tony Campolo, American professor of sociology and author)*

Healthy attitudes

How do we develop healthy ways of thinking about money that will please God?

Learn contentment

'[G]odliness with contentment is great gain. For we brought nothing into the world, and we can take nothing out of it. But if we have food and clothing, we will be content with that' (1 Tim. 6.6–8). Even in Paul's day there were some who saw godliness as a key to unlocking wealth; instead, Paul insists that there's a greater profit in 'godliness with contentment'. Contentment, in a nutshell, is about wanting what you have, not having everything you want. It does not come easy to us! Even Paul had to *learn* to be content. But all our striving will be worth the attainment of an inner peace that accepts whatever God provides for us, knowing his plans are perfect. Hebrews 13.5 tells us: 'Keep your lives free from the love of money and be content with what you have, because God has said, "Never will I leave you; never will I forsake you." ' Money can never hold us, comfort us or tell us we're loved, though we may use it to try to buy or show love.

Do not be proud

'Command those who are rich in this present world not to be arrogant' (1 Tim. 6.17a). One of the most powerful biblical passages about money, Deuteronomy 8.12–14, warns against the spiritual pride that can come from wealth: 'when you eat and are satisfied, when you build fine houses and settle down, and when your herds and flocks grow large and your silver and gold increase and all you have is multiplied, then your heart will become proud and you will forget the LORD your God.' It's all too easy to feel that success and worth are linked to designer clothes, smart cars, exclusive homes or top jobs. But God does not value us according to our status, occupation, income or assets. He looks at our hearts.

Enjoy and be thankful

'[God] richly provides us with everything for our enjoyment' (1 Tim. 6.17). Our appreciation of the world is as individual as our fingerprints: we may delight in a quiet evening walk or, like Steve, in traversing the Cuillin Ridge on the Isle of Skye! Being grateful for the sources of pleasure in our lives – and the money that makes some of them possible – is key. As the lovely French proverb expresses it, 'gratitude is the heart's memory'. If one of the seductions of wealth is that we forget the Lord our God, then gratitude is a powerful way of recalling his provision in our day-to-day lives. A psychology professor conducted an experiment with her students: half were to record five things they were grateful for each week, the rest nothing. The first group reported higher levels of well-being. Maybe we all need to try this experiment!

Be rich in good works

'Command them to do good, to be rich in good deeds' (1 Tim. 6.18). The right attitude to money includes the intention to do the right thing with it. In C. S. Lewis's *The Lion, the Witch and the Wardrobe*, the Pevensie children are told by Father Christmas that their gifts are 'tools not toys'. Similarly, God has entrusted us with gifts to enjoy and tools to use for his glory – not merely for our own pleasure but also to help relieve the needs of others.

Give generously

'Command them to . . . be generous and willing to share' (1 Tim. 6.18). A now retired archbishop once attended a communion service in his diocese and heard the vicar say as he held up the offering plate: 'No matter what we say or do, this is what we think of you.' These are not the usual liturgical words at this point in the service, but an important theological point was made. What we give to God in worship and for the ministry and mission of his Church is a true reflection of our relationship with him.

Healthy lifestyle

Having looked at some helpful attitudes to money, what are the practical things we can do in order to stay financially fit and spiritually healthy around money?

Dream the right dreams

Web article

Can these dry bones live? Planning our financial goals

What dreams do you think God might have for your life? These may come to light as you prayerfully and carefully plan your financial goals. Writing them down, talking them through and then working towards them can be a very liberating experience. Imagine the shared purpose if engaged couples or families were to ask each other, 'What do we want money to do for us in the next few years?' Or the rejigging of spending priorities if you dream of travelling the world or serving God in Africa after early retirement. Knowing our financial goals gives us something to aim at and helps us determine whether any item of major expenditure fits in with our priorities.

Decide how you're going to live

It's not only trying to keep up with the Joneses that can be a problem. What we see on TV sets much of our lifestyle expectations. Now a world without *Doctor Who* or *Match of the Day* is unthinkable, but in 2008 we each watched an average of 26 hours and 12 minutes of TV every week, including an average of 43 adverts. Alongside ordinary people in popular soaps, we're bombarded with images of attractive people living lavish lifestyles, exotic holiday destinations, and personal and home makeover shows – all of which can make us feel we really should be aspiring to more than we have. It's undoubtedly a challenge for each of us to work out an appropriate level of expenditure. But bringing things before God in prayer will definitely help.

Many people buy things they don't need with money they don't have to impress people they don't like!

Learn your money story

Our attitude to money is likely to have been strongly influenced by our childhood and formative experiences. Working out why we feel anxious, fearful, easygoing,

Web article

Written on our hearts: Learning to tell our money stories

11

cautious or foolish around money can be extremely enlightening. It may be helpful to talk to a trusted friend, minister, or even to become part of a small group at church concerned with discipleship around money.

Conclusion

In one way it would be easier if the biblical teaching on money and possessions were simply to give it all away! Precisely that challenge is put by Jesus to the rich ruler in Mark 10.17–22. But it's not the only option the Bible offers for being faithful with money. Old Testament heroes such as Abraham, Solomon and Job were wealthy men, and it was women of substance who supported Jesus' own ministry. Levi threw a party after he'd left everything to follow Jesus, while Zacchaeus was commended for giving away just half of his wealth. And though the early Church held all things in common, they met in the homes of members who presumably still owned them. It seems clear that we're called to be faithful stewards of the good things God has entrusted to us. That stewardship will be characterized by gratitude and contentment, by trust and joy, by generosity and sharing. We will handle our money and possessions not as our own but as the things of God, knowing that in the light of eternity they have no value save how we use them for God's purpose in a hurting world.

> 'Everything which hinders us from loving God above all things and acts as a barrier between ourselves and our obedience to Jesus is our treasure and the place where our heart is.'
> (Dietrich Bonhoeffer, 1906–45, German theologian)

Questions to consider

1 If you had a windfall of £100,000 today, how do you think you'd respond?

2 How much do you think the following influence your lifestyle and spending patterns: friends' and neighbours' standards of living; TV, newspapers, magazines and advertisements?

3 Do you think God would have you alter your lifestyle in any way? If so, how?

4 Which of your possessions takes up most of your emotional and physical energy?

5 How do you feel when you're 'nudged' to give away money or possessions to someone in need?

6 Do you feel comfortable with better-off and less-well-off Christians?

2

Working out a budget

W e've explored some biblical principles for handling money and possessions. Now the first step on our journey to financial freedom and responsible stewardship is to prepare a household budget. Budgeting enables us to take control of our finances and is enormously helpful for three reasons. First, because we cannot be good managers if we don't know what we're managing. Second, because we need to plan for times in life when more resources are needed, such as when we get married (or divorced), when a child is born, when a teenager goes to college or when we're made redundant or retire. Third, because we simply cannot exclude something as important as our wealth and possessions from our discipleship.

'A budget tells your money where to go; otherwise you wonder where it went.'
(J. Edgar Hoover, 1895–1972, Director FBI)

Of course, budgeting isn't a new idea. The older women in Steve's Liverpool parish coped with the depression, the 1941 blitz, rationing and low incomes using nothing more sophisticated than jam jars or tobacco tins on the mantelpiece. Today we might use internet banking rather than jam jars, but the principle is the same: a budget takes control of money. However, it's estimated that around a third of adults in the

UK never budget or plan their finances, and if we belong to the two-thirds who do, we devote only five minutes a week to the task. Think how much time we spend watching TV by comparison!

Let's look in a little more detail at why budgets are important.

A budget tells the truth

In the UK, around five million adults spend more than they earn, and nine million only just break even. Often people are reluctant to prepare a budget because they're afraid: we don't know where our money goes because we don't look, and we don't look because we really don't want to know. But being so vague with our resources is neither spiritually nor practically sound.

A budget puts you in control

People often fear that budgeting will bring loss of personal freedom, but living by a budget actually makes your money go further, and that's always good news. When we fail to budget, there's frequently 'too much month left at the end of the money'. Sensible budgeting will result in less stress and less debt.

A budget says how much is enough

Left to our own devices, enough is always 'a little bit more'; a budget reveals how much *is* enough. It tells us what we need to live on and how much it costs to do the things we want to do. A budget is a *commitment strategy*. When all our emotions are saying, 'Buy this', 'Get that', 'Put it on the card', a budget helps us balance expenditure with income, and to spend on the things we've set as our priorities.

A budget is needed to show to creditors

If you have debts, you may need to prepare a debt-repayment schedule. All the people you owe money to, your creditors, will need to see and agree to this plan. A good budget is essential because promising to repay more than you can afford will just add to your difficulties.

A budget manages God's money

A budget is a spiritual as well as a practical tool: it reminds us we're not managing 'our money' but a *gift* entrusted to us by God. A budget can help us to identify unhelpful

> **Web article**
>
> Beyond Jordan:
> A biblical perspective
> on budgets

attitudes towards money and recognize any unthinking assumptions we may have made in the past. A budget also provides us with the means to express trust, gratitude and generosity through regular, generous giving in proportion to our income.

The 12 days of Stressmas!

If you're still not convinced you really need to budget, why not have a go at the Christmas planner on the website? Imagine you're a

> **Web article**
>
> On the 12th day:
> A budget for Christmas

'nuclear' family – mum, dad and two children. First, quickly guess the total extra amount you think you'll spend over Christmas and New Year. Then work on a Christmas budget. How do the final results compare with your guesstimate? You'll probably be amazed at the gap between what you thought you'd spend and the actual figure. Christmas is the tipping point into debt and money worry for many families: just one-third of us budget for it, but nearly three-quarters admit to Christmas overspending, often because of last-minute panic buying. The plastic and the overdraft take the strain, at interest rates between 20 and 30 per cent and sometimes even higher.

Keeping a record of spending

Obviously, a budget is only useful if it accurately reflects your spending habits. For example, if you're eating three Mars Bars a day and not recording them, then your budget is likely to be pounds out (and you're likely to be pounds heavier!) by the end of the month. We suggest that all members of the household who are old enough to be responsible keep a record of spending for a fortnight or a month. An example is shown in Table 2.1. The first time Steve kept a record of spending, he felt disciplined, virtuous and just a little self-righteous – for a few days. But a new tyre here, a coffee there and a few trips to the cash machine, and it was back to the usual chaos. Welcome to 'miscellaneous'!

Keep your record of spending as simple as possible. You can exclude regular bill payments if you know money is safely set aside for them or if they're paid by standing order or direct

Table 2.1 A record of monthly spending

Monday, [date]				
Item	*Cash (£)*	*Debit card (£)*	*Credit card (£)*	*Cheque (£)*
Coffee with Andy and Jayne	6.70			
New tyre for the car		32.60		
Leaving-collection for Jill at work	5			
Birthday present for nephew John			20	
Deposit for Mary's school trip				10
Subtotal	*11.70*	*32.60*	*20*	*10*
Debit card (£)	*32.60*	<u>Notes</u>		
Credit card (£)	*20*			
Cheque (£)	*10*			
Total (£)	*74.30*			

20

debit. Your record of spending really needs to record those *variable* items, such as food and clothes, and occasional items such as a deposit on a school trip or a spontaneous gift. Record all such payments you make from a debit or credit card and note especially what happens to the cash you draw from the cash machine. The big-ticket items do matter, but it's important to stay in control of the small amounts as well. As the old saying goes: take care of the pennies and the pounds will take care of themselves. The financially free manage money by design, not by default.

Your first estimated budget

The next task is to prepare your first budget. Table 2.2 shows an example of a budget planner from the website (that of the Spender family) to give

Web article

Painting by numbers: A budget planner

an idea of what a first estimated budget might look like.[3]

Hints on preparing your first budget

1 A first step is to get your paperwork in order – gas bills, bank statement, Council Tax and so on. This may be hard at first, but if you develop a simple system for all your financial records it will save time and worry in the future. Check your bank, store and credit card statements for items paid monthly, quarterly or annually. If you don't have a bank account or don't pay many bills through the bank, look carefully at your bills. Check your record of spending for the variables.

2 The budget planner has two columns for income. The first column should be used for your first estimated budget. The second column is for adjusting your budget, which we look at below. In this first estimated budget, if money is tight include only the *minimum debt repayments* you're required

Table 2.2 An example of a budget planner

STEP 1	Income monthly (£)	Income monthly revised (£)
Wages or salary (take home)	1,750.00	1,750.00
Partner's wages or salary (take home)	325.00	488.00
Tips or commission		
Other earnings (net)		
Maintenance or child support		
State/private/work pension(s)		
Income Support		
Jobseeker's Allowance		
Sickness Benefits (e.g. IB, ESA and SSP)		
Working Tax Credit		
Child Tax Credit	45.00	45.00
Child Benefit	87.00	87.00
Housing Benefit/Council Tax Benefit		
Interest		
Boarders or lodgers		
Other benefit income		
Contribution from children	20.00	
[1] Total income	2,207.00	2,390.00

STEP 2 Housing costs/utilities	Outgoings monthly (£)	Outgoings monthly revised (£)
Mortgage payment	750.00	750.00
Rent		
Mortgage endowment payments		
Second mortgage/other secured loans		
Council Tax	140.00	140.00
Water rates	29.00	29.00
Service charge or ground rent		
Buildings/contents house insurance	40.00	40.00
Life insurance		
Gas	65.00	65.00
Electricity	40.00	40.00
Other fuel costs		
Other possible priority items		
Maintenance or child support payments		
Court fines		
Hire purchase/conditional sale		
TV rental/licence	12.00	12.00
County Court Judgements (CCJ)		
Tax/National Insurance (non-PAYE)		
[2] Total housing and priority items	1,076.00	1,076.00

STEP 3
Other important items

	Outgoings monthly (£)	Outgoings monthly revised (£)
Religious and charitable giving	150.00	150.00
Home phone and mobile phone(s)	130.00	110.00
Pension/AVC payments		
Other		
[3] Total other items	280.00	260.00

STEP 4
Everyday expenditure

	Outgoings monthly (£)	Outgoings monthly revised (£)
Food and drink/housekeeping	400.00	400.00
Newspapers and magazines	60.00	15.00
Public transport (work, school, shopping)	55.00	15.00
Car road tax	14.00	14.00
Fuel (petrol, diesel, oil etc.)	100.00	100.00
Car insurance	30.00	30.00
Car service, MOT, repairs, breakdown cover	25.00	25.00
Childcare, pocket money, school trips	25.00	25.00
School meals and meals at work	100.00	30.00
Pets (food and vet's bills, insurance)	35.00	35.00
Cigarettes and tobacco		
Clothes and footwear	45.00	45.00
Household items (repairs, replacements etc.)		
Health costs (e.g. dentist, optician)	20.00	20.00
Alcohol	60.00	20.00
Other 2		
Other 3		
[4] Total everyday expenditure	969.00	774.00

(continued overleaf)

Table 2.2 (*continued*)

STEP 5 Other expenditure	Outgoings monthly (£)	Outgoings monthly revised (£)
Entertaining, eating out	35.00	35.00
Holidays	80.00	60.00
Savings		
Gardening		
Hobbies/leisure/sport/gym etc.	20.00	20.00
Gifts (e.g. birthdays)	20.00	20.00
Christmas presents etc.	40.00	20.00
Courses and professional fees		
Credit card payments		
Loan repayments		
Catalogue payments		
Other 1		
Other 2		
Other 3		
[5] Total other expenditure	195.00	155.00

STEP 6	monthly (£)	revised (£)
[BOX 1] Total income	2,207.00	2,390.00
[BOX 2] Housing costs/priority items	1,076.00	1,076.00
[BOX 3] Other important items	280.00	260.00
[BOX 4] Everyday expenditure	969.00	774.00
[BOX 5] Other expenditure	195.00	155.00
[6] Total outgoings (= BOX 2,3,4, & 5)	2,520.00	2,265.00
Money left over BOX 1 minus BOX 6	−313.00	125.00

to make on any personal loans, store or credit card borrowing. You *must* make those payments or you'll store up trouble and increase your debts. Once you know what surplus of income over expenditure is available to repay any debts faster, then you can allocate additional payments. Of course, if you're already comfortably making higher repayments then enter these figures.

3 Prepare your budget according to your **pattern of income.** If you're paid weekly prepare a weekly budget; if you're paid monthly prepare a monthly budget.

4 The budget planner has many **categories** to help jog your memory in case you've overlooked any spending. You'll almost certainly not be spending in every category.

5 Make your budget **simple.** If you have a monthly budget, pay all the bills you can monthly. For quarterly bills (e.g. gas) budget for one-third of their estimated cost each month. Similarly, divide any annual payments by 12 and again put that figure in your monthly budget. This is money that you have but cannot spend because you have to set it aside until the bill falls due.

6 **Council Tax** is tricky because it's usually collected over 10 months not 12. We suggest you divide the total bill by ten but allocate that amount to all 12 months. That way you make sure you pay the bill in ten months but have two months 'bonus' income. It may be possible to get your local council to spread the payments over 12 months.

7 If you're not confident or if the maths scares you off, **don't be too embarrassed or too proud** to ask for help from someone you trust.[4]

Determining whether your budget is in surplus or deficit

Once your first estimated budget is complete, you'll need to add up your total expenditure and deduct it from your total income – the spreadsheet on the website will do that for you. If your income is more than you spend, you have permission to feel relieved! Many of us, however, will have the nasty surprise of discovering that we're currently spending more each month than we earn. In fact the overspending may be considerable. If this is your situation, please do not despair, as we'll soon be looking at ways of rectifying it. However, if you're at all uneasy, contact one of the debt advice agencies at the end of Chapter 4, on dealing with debt, or see the website.

Adjusting your budget

What do you do if current spending – including giving, savings, debt repayments and everyday expenditure – adds up to more than your current income? Quite simply, to balance your budget you must increase your income and/or reduce your expenditure. When the Spender family completed their first budget (see Table 2.2), they discovered they were spending £313 more each month than their income. They had to work on adjusting their budget so that it balanced (see the second column for income and expenditure, headed 'revised').

Increasing your income

There are some obvious things to look at, such as:

- ensuring you're receiving your full entitlement to benefits;
- checking your tax code and your eligibility for Tax Credits;
- ensuring you're receiving proper maintenance from a former partner.

You might also consider renting out a spare room to a student, or working freelance (perhaps turning a hobby into a money-making concern) or increasing the hours you spend at your regular job. The Spender family planned to augment their income by £183 a month. Mum would do an additional half-day a week part-time secretarial work (bringing in £163), and the teenage daughter agreed to chip in £20 towards her mobile phone.

When you've looked at all the ways you can think of to increase your income, add the new figures to the revised column in Step 1, and put the total in the box. (You'll see that the Spender family's income is now £2,390.) Put your total income in the 'revised' column in Step 6.

Reducing your spending

How might you reduce your spending? The Spender family managed to cut theirs down by £255 a month almost without noticing. Dad took sandwiches to work (saving £70) and walked there as well (£40 not spent on bus fares and a free workout!). The family reduced their Christmas spending budget by £20, and indulged in fewer drinks at the weekly pub quiz (saving £40 a month). They stopped their newspapers (another £45 saved), and did not renew a mobile phone contract that cost £20 a month. They also decided on a less expensive holiday, reducing their usual budget by £20 a month.

A couple of questions to have in mind at all times are: Is this really needed? And if it is: Can I buy it somewhere else more cheaply? Some hints are available at <www.moneybasics. co.uk/>. Here are a few more:

- **Utilities:** Use price-comparison sites or ring around to get gas and electricity for less. Pay by direct debit if you can. It is surely morally wrong, but those without bank accounts pay more for their utilities.
- **Telecoms:** Review your TV, phone and broadband package. A ten-minute phone call saved one family £40 per month for the same service! Is mobile internet access absolutely essential? Downgrading your TV bundle might save you £20 a month. If this were invested over five years at a gross interest rate of 3 per cent, you'd save over £1,000 – enough to pay cash to replace several worn-out appliances.

- **Food:** Never try to balance a budget by going hungry, but do keep an eye open for special offers. It definitely pays to be a canny shopper.
- **Lifestyle:** Over £200 million is wasted each year on unused gym memberships alone. A family of four that eats out once a week for £40 and switches to eating out one week in four could save £120 a month – and making an additional repayment of £120 on your mortgage would save thousands in interest, and pay off the mortgage several years earlier.

How are you doing?

When you enter and add up your revised outgoings, are you left with a surplus? If so, well done! If not, don't give up – with commitment and patience you *will* get there. Making your first budget takes time, but as the first and most important step in taking control over your money, it's well worth the effort.

Ensuring your budget works

The following steps will help you to make sure your budget works for you in practice, not just on paper.

1 Develop a simple system

It's a good idea to have one bank account from which you make all your regular payments, and to pay as much as possible by standing order and direct debit (which are often cheaper than paying by cheque or cash). You might decide to set up another account for Christmas expenses, holiday savings, a monthly clothes allowance or car tax and maintenance. Many banks and building societies offer linked savings accounts, but do keep things as simple as possible or you'll make mistakes.

2 Don't forget 'hidden' bills

These are always expenses that occur on an annual or irregular basis, and you must budget for these or you could be in trouble.

For example, a car MOT is an annual expense, with both a fixed (the test itself) and a variable cost (if the car requires work to pass). The amount needed – which for repairs is always a guesstimate – should be divided by 12 and set aside every month. Other bills commonly overlooked are insurance premiums (buildings and contents, if these apply, and assuming you're not already paying them monthly by direct debit), annual subscriptions and, for the self-employed, various taxes. On top of these, remember that many domestic appliances need replacing over time, and most don't give warning when they're about to give up.

3 Control impulse spending

Impulse items are those things that grab our attention when we're out shopping and mostly get paid for with credit cards. To avoid busting the budget, you might ask the following questions: Would I buy this item if I had to pay with hard cash? Is this purchase a genuine need or a reasonable want, or am I spending to make myself feel better? Could I go home, sleep on it and still want this in the morning? You might miss a genuine bargain by waiting, but it's much more likely you'll save money.

4 Plan your gift buying

Presents for Christmas, birthdays, a colleague's retirement or friends moving all need to be planned for. Think of the total amount you can afford to spend during the year and then make sure to keep to it. Draw up your calendar of birthday and Christmas gifts and allocate the sum of money according to your preferences.

5 Watch miscellaneous spending

We often hear people say, 'I just don't know where the money goes – so I put it in '"miscellaneous"'. As you budget, your aim is virtually to remove 'miscellaneous' as a category and work out where everything you spend really does go. However, you may find it comforting, at the beginning at least, to allocate to 'miscellaneous' a fixed amount of spending money each week – cash you keep in your pocket. Once it's gone, it's gone. Resist the urge to pop back to the cash machine, just for a 'tenner'. Your bank statement will tell you how many times you visit a cash machine – and how much those small withdrawals add up to!

6 Accept responsibility in the home

If you're single, you're probably your own bookkeeper. However, where two or more people are responsible for the running of the household budget, it's important to work out who does what. Deciding on where money should be spent has to be agreed (and is likely to involve a fair amount of compromise), but once agreed, all parties must be willing to keep to the planned budget. It will cause tension if one individual repeatedly or casually exceeds agreed expenditure.

7 Keep good records

It's impossible to manage your money without accurate records. Make sure you have a simple system for storing your bills and recording your payments, and review your bank statements each month to stay on top of things. Computer software can help you keep track of your money, and internet banking gives you immediate access to your accounts. But paper still works well!

8 Set family goals

It's always much easier to work at something, for example saving for a holiday, if you're all pulling in the same direction. Having future goals helps everybody to understand why certain things are happening, and we'll now explore how you might do this.

Setting your financial goals

Like the dry bones that Ezekiel saw in the valley, a budget needs something to breathe life into it, something to make it live. That's exactly what planning your financial goals will do. You may want to clear your unsecured debts in five years, help a child through college or save up for that twenty-fifth wedding-anniversary holiday. You set the destination – for the immediate future, the mid term and the long term – and your budget will map the way to get there. Look at the example in Table 2.3.

Table 2.3 An example of a set of financial goals

Names: Charles and Catherine	**Date:** 1 January 2010

Giving goals
We'd like to increase our giving to 10 per cent of income this year, and over five years to 15 per cent.

Other giving goals
To sponsor one needy child through Tearfund and to help support a missionary regularly.

Debt-repayment goals
We'd like to pay off the following debts:

Credit card: £1,130; in the next 12 months
Car loan: £3,200; within 3 years

In the long term, we'd like to reduce our mortgage by overpaying to the equivalent of making 13 mortgage payments each year. We will not take out any new credit commitments other than for a real emergency.

Emergency savings
We have no emergency savings, so we'll pay £10 each week into the credit union[5] this year: £500+.

Educational goals
We'd like to set aside money to help our child's (Jen's) higher education:

Person	College	Annual contribution	Total cost
Jen	University	£1,500	£4,500

Savings goals
We'd like to save 7.5 per cent of our after-tax income.
Other savings goals: to increase this to 10 per cent in 5 years.

Table 2.3 (*continued*)

Put aside £100 a month for Christmas.
In four years' time we'd like to celebrate our 25th wedding anniversary with a special holiday.

Investments
We'd like to make the following investments:

Retirement plan: £1,500 per year

We'd also like to provide Jen with our home, free of mortgage, and also a cash gift of £5,000.

We'd also like to leave a legacy to the church and to Tearfund.

One-off purchases
We'd like to make the following purchases in the next 12 months:

Double-glazed front door: £600
Get new refrigerator: £400

Lifestyle and income
We'd like jointly to achieve the following annual income, now that Charles has gained his new qualification at work and Catherine wants to work full time again: £45,000.

Writing a budget statement

A budget and our financial goals are always linked to our actual and desired standard of living. But the Bible does not prescribe one standard of living for everyone, so each of us has to work out what's right just for us. What do you see as your God-given standard of living? You might find that Karen's and Ken's statement helps your thinking:

We're happy living in our present house and have no desire to move to a larger one, but we'd like to add a conservatory. Our main aims are to see our children through university, clear our mortgage and both give and save an extra five per cent of income each year. Ken wishes to retire at 60 and then work voluntarily for the church. We intend to change our car every seven years, buying a low-mileage, used car as a replacement. Although we want to remain smart, we do not intend to follow too many fashions. We want to help our children become financially mature, but we especially want to put God first in all aspects of our finances.

If you're in a relationship or share a household with others, we suggest you each write your own separate budget statement and then compare notes before working together on a shared statement.

An assets and liabilities statement

Once you're comfortable with preparing and living with a budget, there's another important and helpful step you can take to put you in control of

Web article

Assets, liabilities and net worth

money. A budget deals only with cash coming in and going out, with income and expenditure. But money is more than cash. We also have, first, our 'assets', things we own that have monetary value. A house is an asset if we own it, so too is a car, cash saved in the bank, shares, jewellery, a time-share or that most prized earthly possession, a season ticket at Goodison Park. Second, we also have our 'liabilities', that is, money we owe others. Such debts may include credit cards, outstanding loans or hire-purchase arrangements and a mortgage, if we have one. So another important step in taking control of our finances is to draw up an *assets and liabilities statement* (see Table 2.4, overleaf), which lists what we have and what we owe.

When we have taken our liabilities away from our assets, we have, in financial terms, our 'total net worth'. An example may help. Let's say you borrow a sum of £6,000 to buy a second-hand car. The car is now an asset that you own; if you sold it you would get money for it. After 18 months you still owe £4,000 on the car; that is, you have a £4,000 liability – money you owe to someone else. But after 18 months the car itself is worth no more than £3,000 – its value drops faster than you

Table 2.4 An assets and liabilities statement

Assets	Market value	Assets	Market value
Home		Shares/ investments	
Car/motorbike/ bicycle		Cash value of life insurance/ endowments	
Caravan/second home/time-share		Collectables, e.g. stamps/ coins/pictures	
Computer/ printer/laptop		Jewellery	
Furniture		Pension plan	
Consumer goods, e.g. TV		Other assets 1	
Cash savings		Other assets 2	
Total value of assets			

Liabilities	Amount owed	Minimum payment
Mortgage		
Utility arrears debts		
Income tax/National Insurance		
Council Tax arrears		
Credit/hire-purchase arrangements		
Credit cards		
Store cards		
Overdrafts		
Credit-union loans		
Loans		
Personal debts – family and friends		
Other 'secured' loans		
Other 'unsecured' loans		
Net worth (total assets less total liabilities)		

make repayments. So you have an asset worth £3,000 but a liability of £4,000. At the moment, your total net worth is negative by £1,000. But in your shed is a vintage British motorbike, worth £1,800 and the object of rather too much love and attention. So now your total net worth is a positive £800.

Getting practical

Your first statement does not need to be too precise. Just estimate the amount of each major asset and liability. Seeing in black and white just how much we owe can be quite frightening, but it's vitally important to list everything: credit cards, hire-purchase arrangements, credit-union loans, store cards, borrowing from family and so on.

It's a good idea to review your assets and liabilities statement on a yearly basis to see what significant trends are taking place, and to add in any major new purchases or commitments. A review of assets and liabilities isn't just for people in debt. Over time our needs and situations change, and it's good stewardship to review our position. For example, a four-bedroom house may have been suitable when three children lived at home, but in retirement it may be time to downsize, release capital and reduce expenditure.

Surrendering everything to God

Like a budget, an assets and liabilities statement is a financial tool with a spiritual purpose: it reminds us that everything we 'own' in fact belongs to God. At the bottom of your statement, you might like to add wording along the lines of the example given overleaf.

On 20 April 2010, we surrender to God the ownership of all our assets and no longer claim them as our own. We hold them in trust from God to be enjoyed fully and shared generously. We acknowledge our liabilities, trust God's provision for them and commit to working towards reducing our debts and living a sustainable lifestyle.

Signed ....

....
(Stewards of the above)

Questions to consider

1 Why are we not all called to have the same things or standard of living?
2 How ambitious can I be about what I **want to have**?
3 Do I ever feel guilty about my standard of living?
4 Should my living standards rise automatically because my income has increased?
5 How do I/we make spending decisions?
6 What influences me to make certain purchases?
7 Do I always differentiate between needs and wants?

3

The problem of credit

Since the mid 1970s, when the rules governing consumer credit were relaxed, there's been an explosion in personal borrowing. The first credit card was launched in 1966; by the end of 2008 there were over 146 million debt, credit or charge cards. That's nearly four per person, and until the credit crunch, a staggering 84 per cent of credit card applications were accepted with no proof of income required. In the 1970s, the debt-to-income ratio was 70 per cent; in 2005 it was 140 per cent. In 2010, 'debt freedom day' fell on 20 February. We worked the first 50 days of the year just to pay off the interest on our debts. On 21 February we started paying off the debt itself!

But what the banks lent to us they had themselves borrowed from large companies and financial institutions, many from overseas. By 2008, UK private and public borrowing was around £4,000 billion, just over 300 per cent of our Gross Domestic Product. When the credit bonanza was good it was very good. But things began to turn bad in late summer 2007. Concern over investment in the US sub-prime mortgage market contributed to the first run on a UK bank in 100 years, as customers rushed to withdraw their money from Northern Rock, fearing it was about to become insolvent. Northern Rock was nationalized, but Lehman Brothers, a year later, was allowed to fail, resulting in governments across the world pouring money into the banking systems to stave off total collapse.

Much has been done to restore stability, but at enormous cost. Ordinary people have lost their jobs or their homes, seen little return on lifetime savings, and watched their pension funds plunge into a black hole.

A rose by any other name

Our attitude towards borrowing is vastly different from that of our grandparents, who had a horror of being in debt. But what used to be thought of as debt has been cleverly repackaged as 'credit', and we're now encouraged to think of borrowing as a way of enriching personal and family life. Obviously, most of us need a bank or building society loan to buy a house, but it can be tempting then to borrow against the value of a mortgaged home to fund the lifestyle we aspire to. It's common to use credit for relatively large purchases, like a car or new furniture, and almost impossible to shop online without a card to hand. Even picking up a few gifts at a department store involves being offered a discount if we take a store card. With society anxious to take 'the waiting out of wanting', it's little wonder so many of us succumb to the pressure of borrowing. In fact there's so much debt in this country that Mr Average has been described as someone driving on a government bond-financed road, in a bank-financed car, fuelled by credit card-financed petrol, going to buy store card-financed furniture to put in his mortgage-financed house.

> *Give yourself five minutes to think of all the different types of credit available in the UK. Then tick off the ones that you've used yourself.*

Credit where it's due

Now credit can be very convenient – both of us have credit cards. They make for easy payment, allow an interest-free period and smooth cash flow. They can turn the cost of a large, one-off purchase into smaller, more manageable payments. In fact, half of credit card holders pay off their balance in full each month, and there are many people who never or rarely use credit. Others play the system, looking for introductory low or zero interest rates for purchases and balance transfers, though such 'rate tarts' have become quite rare.

You may be asking yourself, What's the problem? While it's true that credit is debt, you're not *in debt* until you miss a payment. A bill that's due (e.g.

Web article

Servant to the lender:
The problem of credit

for electricity) wouldn't be considered a debt if paid on time. So does credit deserve a bad press? Or is it all right for Christians to borrow money? Let's consider some biblical and practical principles.

Bible questions to consider

Proverbs 22.7 tells us, 'The rich rule over the poor, and the borrower is servant to the lender.' We should be cautious about credit because borrowing binds us to the lender and

Web article

Remember the Lord:
Wealth as gift, obligation
and temptation

to an uncertain future, while Romans 13.8 tells us not to owe anyone anything. But the Bible doesn't condemn all borrowing (Deut. 15.1–3; Matt. 5.42), and Jesus criticizes the one who will not cancel debts (Matt. 18.23–35). The Bible has three broad perspectives on wealth and possessions that help us to think through the question of borrowing.

Say we plan to borrow to go on holiday. A pertinent question would be, Is this holiday likely to give us a sense of *gift* or *blessing*? A once-in-a-lifetime trip to Disneyland while the children are young is one thing, a luxurious annual vacation we feel we deserve but cannot afford may turn out to be no blessing at all.

We should also ask about the possible *temptation* attached to a purchase. Do we genuinely need a new car for work or family reasons, or are we splashing out because we're a bit embarrassed about the one we're driving at the moment? Put simply, will the car serve a purpose or make a statement? Finally, what *obligations* might a purchase bring? Most obviously there's the obligation to make regular repayments, but there are others as well. Keith and his wife Sue once bought a new three-piece suite, and that very evening a member of their home group spilt a cup of coffee on it. Was Keith more embarrassed for that person than he was upset about the sofa? (Keith says he's repented of one of the emotions he felt!) A home comes with the obligation of hospitality, a car with the obligation to share, wealth with the obligation to be generous.

Personal questions to consider

Here are three other personal questions to ask before considering credit:

1 Will borrowing for this item put me under **financial strain**? Ideally, the repayments should be quite manageable on your budget.
2 Will borrowing for this item put me under **emotional strain**? Are you likely to become anxious or stressed? Will borrowing from your family or a friend cause particular problems? Is it likely to change how you feel towards them? There's a powerful warning on how debt can affect the way we regard others in the parable of the unforgiving servant (Matt. 18.23–35).
3 Will borrowing for this item put me under **giving strain**? If borrowing money means we cannot give God the 'first fruits' of our income, we should not take on the loan.

Practical guidelines for considering credit

- Do you have a clear intention to repay the loan – and a realistic plan?
- Are you borrowing to finance a genuine need? Emergencies in that category might include a broken washing machine, school clothes for the children or repairs to a car needed for work.
- Will the item or experience be of lasting value? Historically, homes have been a good investment in monetary terms, but there are other kinds of worth. An experience can have significant emotional or relational value. Careful, planned borrowing might make possible a once-in-a-lifetime anniversary celebration, or work on a garden that's the focus of someone's leisure.
- Does the value of the item being purchased significantly exceed the amount being borrowed? An example would be having a healthy deposit when buying a house or a car that is worth more than you actually pay for it.

And now, a final brief checklist.

Have I really thought things through?

It's easy to be influenced by slick advertising and find yourself making an important financial decision when you haven't really considered the consequences. Discussing with others can be helpful, so don't be embarrassed to consult family and friends, or even professional advisers.

Have I done enough research?

Evaluate all the options carefully. It's vital to check if the annual percentage rate of interest (APR) you're being offered is affordable. Ask about penalty clauses for late or missed

Web article

Credit Street: An overview of credit options

43

payments, and about any early repayment charges in case you want to pay the loan off quickly. Although many loans offer a particularly low level of repayment, the length of time you're tied into it will determine how much you pay altogether. Also remember that some loans are *secured* loans – they're secured against your home, and you risk losing it if you fail to keep up with the payments. Always read the small print – the devil is usually hidden away in the detail for obvious reasons. As someone said, 'the big print giveth and the small print taketh away'.

Is my purchase really affordable?

Always ensure you have the money available to repay the loan. Ask yourself questions such as: Could I afford the repayments if interest rates rose sharply? What happens if I lose my job or become ill? Do I have life or sickness insurance in place to protect me? (Do be cautious about payment protection plans, often sold alongside loans: there are real concerns about the cost of this insurance, as well as about how much cover it actually provides.) Take out the loan only if you're happy with your answers.

We're now going to spend some time considering two major credit purchases: buying a house and buying a car.

Buying a house

Owning our own home is something many of us aspire to. However, the decision whether – and what – to buy should be based firmly on two things: need and financial ability. We probably all know people who've taken on homes they could not really afford, either to keep up with their friends or live in a good neighbourhood with well-performing schools, or because they seemed great investments. These are understandable pressures, but it really does make sense to buy a house within your budget.

It may be that you have to settle for a smaller house than you'd like, or one in a less desirable area. However, the less you owe on your mortgage, the quicker you can pay it off, freeing resources to help your children through university, enjoy during your retirement – or any number of other things. Though your financial situation will be the main consideration in determining what type of house you go for, there are other factors to weigh up.

- Is your job secure enough for you to take on a mortgage? If not, consider renting instead of buying, at least for a while.
- Can you afford the additional expenses involved in buying a property, such as stamp duty and furnishings? You will of course also have the ongoing costs of Council Tax, water rates, electricity, gas and so on.
- Do you plan to live in the same area for some time, say six or more years? If so, buying may be the best option.
- What's the local economy like in the area you're planning to move to? Is the cost of living higher than where you are now? Are houses appreciating in value or are lots for sale?

Understanding equity and deposits

Let's say you've bought a £200,000 house with a £10,000 deposit. The £10,000 is what's called equity, and you've borrowed £190,000. If the market value of your house drops by more than £10,000 – a 5 per cent fall – you'll be in negative equity, which means you owe more than your house is worth. This will put you in an almost impossible position should an emergency occur and you're forced to sell your house. Now you have no equity left in the house – in fact after the sale you may still owe the mortgage company, or their insurers, a significant sum of money, for which they can pursue you for years. If, however, you'd bought the same house and put down a deposit of £30,000, the market would have had to fall enormously before all your equity disappeared. It really is a good idea to save as much as possible before buying, and the best mortgage deals are for those who have a good sized deposit.

What kind of house?

If you've decided to buy, you'll have to consider whether to go for a new or an older property. With older houses there are several advantages. You know exactly what the house is going to cost, and you often get extras such as carpets, curtains, light fittings and some appliances thrown in. On the other hand, older houses are likely to be more expensive to maintain: you may find yourself sorting out problems with the roof, drainage or heating, for example. A basic survey will come as part of the mortgage arrangement, but do consider investing in a more detailed one: it could well save you money in the end.

To sum up, our advice is to:

- start small;
- make your home as attractive as possible;
- sell it as house values and your income increase;
- buy the next sized house;
- downsize to a smaller property when you no longer need as much space, in order to release the value in your home.

Mortgages: fixed, discount and tracker

Most people have a mortgage over 25 years, and the majority of people now opt for a mortgage that has a fixed rate of interest – a rate that doesn't change with the Bank of England base rate. Fixed-rate mortgages are very helpful from a budgeting point of view because you know exactly what you'll be paying month after month. Tracker mortgages are different. They 'track', or follow, the Bank of England base rate – usually by a few percentage points above or below it. The advantage here is that when the base rate falls, the cost of a mortgage also falls, because the bank or building society is committed to tracking the movement of the base rate. But note that the opposite is also true: if rates rise, so do mortgage costs, and that can pose real problems. It's also possible to buy 'discount' mortgages: these offer a discount for a period of time on the so-called standard variable rate (SVR) of your bank or building society, which will often be at least a couple of percentage points higher than the Bank of England base rate. However, you need to be aware that the bank or building society chooses its own SVR: when interest rates fall it may not reduce its SVR, and so you may not see any benefit – unlike in the same situation if you've taken out a tracker mortgage.

Note also that fixed-rate, discount and tracker mortgages are often for a set period of two, three or five years. At the end of the set period you'll almost certainly be put onto the more expensive SVR unless you arrange to remortgage, which can be expensive. Your mortgage provider is obliged in law to provide you with a 'key facts' document that summarizes your mortgage terms in relatively easy terms – you should study this carefully before agreeing to a mortgage.

Mortgages: endowment, repayment or interest-only

There are several different kinds of mortgages. With a repayment mortgage, you pay off both the capital and interest over the period of the mortgage. Each monthly payment goes towards paying off some of the interest on your loan and some of the capital. With an endowment mortgage, you pay back only interest on the loan, but also make payments – usually monthly – into an endowment policy. The hope is that at the end of the term of the mortgage, the endowment policy has matured sufficiently not only to pay off the capital element but also to provide a nest egg. In fact many endowment policies taken out over the last 25 years or so have not proved sufficient even to pay off the mortgage. You should not go for this sort of arrangement without independent professional advice, especially given the poor surrender value of these policies in the early years. An interest-only mortgage is just that: you pay the interest but never reduce the capital, so at the end of the mortgage you still owe the full value of the house. Do take advice if you choose this kind of mortgage. It can help you get onto the property ladder or manage difficult financial circumstances in the short term, but you shouldn't assume your house will increase in value sufficiently – or that Auntie Joy will leave you a handy legacy – to pay off the capital value when the mortgage period is up.

Mortgage insurance

Given that the government has tightened the guidelines on paying Income Support towards mortgage interest, it is sensible to consider taking out insurance that protects you in case of redundancy or sickness, which would mean loss of income.

Refinancing

If interest rates fall after you buy your house, you may well be tempted to switch to a cheaper lender. It's important to work out exactly how much you'd actually be saving, and then compare this with the cost of switching lenders, which might include a cancellation fee, a new title search and a survey. If these expenses are likely to be wiped out over a couple of years, then it probably is worth refinancing.

Second mortgages

People often take out second mortgages to finance some form of home improvement or because they need more money to pay off bills. It pays to be wary, however. Home-improvement loans are secured on your property, and if things go wrong, creditors can go to court to seek repossession. And in any case, if you can't pay your bills, you need to treat the problem itself – so go back to your budget!

Repossessions

After a period of relatively low house repossessions, figures have been rising due to the effects of the credit crunch, increased food and fuel costs and falling house prices. If you get behind on your payments, it's vital you talk to your lender immediately. It's not necessarily in the lender's business interests to repossess your home, and the Government has introduced a voluntary code of conduct that provides some protection for those struggling to pay their mortgage. Draw up a careful budget, with all unnecessary spending stripped out; make an offer to your lender based on what you can afford; and try with all your might to stick to it. If it looks like repossession is inevitable, try to persuade your lender to let you stay in the property while you attempt to sell it. You're likely to get a much better price for it if you're still in residence.

To sum up, it's much better to regard a house as a home rather than as an investment. A small, cosy and comfortable place you can afford is likely to make you much happier in the long term than a large one with half-empty rooms and high maintenance costs. Most people still owe money on their mortgage when they retire – aim to be an exception.

Buying a car

In the UK, around three-quarters of families own at least one car, so it's worth considering some sensible guidelines on purchasing this major item of expenditure – especially as our reasons for buying or changing cars are often emotional rather than rational. Those who buy brand new cars and trade them in for another new model less than four years later usually waste the largest amounts of money. But many of us change our cars because we want to, not because we need to.

Is buying a brand new car the best stewardship of hard-earned money? Costs for a mid-range new car – including payments, insurance and maintenance – frequently exceed £350 a month. Some of us will be able to afford this figure; others may discover there isn't enough money left over for food and clothing. As these are essential items, they may eventually find themselves getting into debt to provide them.

We suggest that the 'average' family needs to buy a good-quality, reliable, *used* car, and that *no more than 18 per cent* of net available income should be allocated to motoring expenses. To summarize:

- honestly evaluate your need for a new car;
- if you must have one, consider a good-quality used car;
- look at the mileage and condition, as well as the price;
- pay cash if possible;
- check you're getting a good trade-in price for your old car – more often than not you'll do better selling it privately.

Challenges

Finally, here are three things for you to consider.

1 Do you take the credit?

Web article

A credit challenge

Take the credit challenge on the website. Answer questions such as, 'How many credit cards do you have?' Or 'What's the total amount you owe on credit?' Then go to your paperwork, check out how accurate your answers are, and list every single line of credit you have – even borrowing from your mum! If you can't quickly lay your hands on your paperwork, or if you don't want to look at it, that's a sign you need to get to grips with your credit.

2 Cash for a month

Our good friends at Care for the Family popularized the idea of putting away the plastic and living on cash for a month. Try it – you're likely to be amazed at what you learn about yourself and your spending habits! Even if you go back to using debit or credit cards, you'll see and do things differently.

3 See how others live

There's an old Native American saying: You don't know someone until you've walked a mile in their moccasins. If you've never used sub-prime credit (loans made to people who wouldn't ordinarily qualify for credit), put yourself in the shoes of those who do:

- compare the prices in a weekly repayment store or catalogue with those where *you* usually shop;
- use a cheque-cashing shop to cash a cheque and see what they charge;
- sell an article at a buyback store (such as Cash Converters) and claim it back within 28 days;
- or just talk to and learn from others in your church or local community who cannot access mainstream credit.

4

Dealing with debt

Over the past 30 years, the incidence of debt has reached epidemic proportions. At the end of 2009, personal debt in the UK stood at £1.46 trillion, and for much of the decade had increased at a rate of £1 million every four to five minutes. As the recession bit deeply in March 2010, Citizens' Advice Bureaux saw 9,500 new debt cases *every day*. Government statistics suggest that 13 per cent of households with borrowing are in arrears on at least one repayment – over three million people.

Behind these grim statistics are the lives of real people. Marriage breakdown, robberies, homes repossessions, desperate individuals driven to depression and, tragically, even suicide, may all be linked to debt. But debt is still largely a hidden problem, and appearances can be deceptive. After Keith had preached at one church, the minister commented that he was glad the sermon had been on money in general rather than on debt, because his parish was in an affluent part of the country where debt wasn't a problem. Keith learned later that 47 copies of his Credit Action debt guide had been given away at the end of the service! And after he'd spoken at a church in London, a very well-dressed lady told him that debt was a subject in which she had a particular interest: six months previously her husband had killed himself the day before their house was due to be repossessed. He was a doctor, and no one dreamed he had any financial problems. In fact, one of the elders later told Keith that if they'd conducted a survey within the church to name the wealthiest person, most people would have assumed it was the doctor. Debt touches people of all social classes.

But no situation, however challenging, is beyond the transforming power of Christ. One of the most amazing experiences of Keith's life took place at an informal evening service in a church in another affluent area. He relates it in his own words.

After I'd spoken, the minister asked, 'Do you really believe debt is a problem in this part of the city?' Looking at the number of people in the church, my reply was simply in the affirmative. The minister found this very hard to believe, but at that moment a young woman stood up and said, 'I'm sorry, but you don't know your congregation very well.' At this point I expected the minister to retire gracefully, but instead he immediately shot himself in the other foot! 'I haven't seen you around for some time, Daisy', he said, to which she replied, 'No, you haven't. But as you know, John and I had a little boy about a year ago and then, a few months later, John lost his job. We found we were in quite substantial debt and started arguing a lot. Eventually things got so bad I took the baby back to my mum's. The reason I haven't been to church recently is because I haven't been able to afford the bus fare, and the reason both John and I are here tonight is because we believe it's our last chance of saving our marriage.' A stunned silence filled the church, and then the most wonderful thing happened. A group of normally reserved British Christians suddenly became the Body of Christ. Some were on their knees in prayer and others were in tears. Both husband and wife were engulfed in hugs, while a number of people quietly got their cheque books open. I watched the Body of Christ – refreshing, restoring, giving hope – and then I went home. I was no longer needed.

A widow's story

The narrative of 2 Kings 4.1–7 is as relevant today as it was thousands of years ago. A widow cannot pay her debts, so the man to whom she owes money takes her two sons as slaves in payment. She goes to Elisha for help and, as a result, God

Web article

Debt in the Bible

miraculously multiplies the small amount of olive oil she owns. Indeed, there's such an abundance that the proceeds are sufficient to pay off all her debts and leave the family enough to live on. When we read this powerful story, we should not rush so quickly to the miracle of the oil that we fail to appreciate the pain of the widow, the compassion of Elisha and the heart of God for the indebted. Dwelling on these things will give us an insight into the causes and the effects of personal debt on our lives.[6]

The debt triggers

The causes of indebtedness are much more complex than simple overspending. The widow's *bereavement* reminds us that two-thirds of us will have got into debt due to an unexpected change, either in our domestic circumstances or in the workplace. Babies – planned or unplanned – can bring much joy and also great deal of expense! The *average* divorce costs around £28,000, and the death of a family's major breadwinner will obviously have severe consequences. Loss of overtime, bonus or commission, as well as redundancy or the failure of a small business, can cause income to take a tumble; sickness or injury can make work impossible. Many debt triggers are beyond our control, and it's precisely the sense of helplessness they arouse that causes so much despair.

The widow has no *economic status*, and this reminds us that the poor are especially susceptible to debt. They have fewer assets, are less able to afford insurance against illness or redundancy and, as we saw in the previous chapter, pay much more for their borrowing. They may fail to claim benefits they're entitled to through lack of information; occasionally they may find that they're not receiving all they should (the UK benefits system isn't infallible). Particularly vulnerable are single parents, 90 per cent of whom are women.

The effects of debt

The widow's distress finds an echo in the experiences of millions today who struggle with debt. Of all the emotions we feel when we're in debt, fear is likely to be uppermost. We may find we just don't have the nerve to open the post, go to the door when the bell rings, answer the phone. We may be terrified of our partner finding out the truth – indeed, issues around debt and money are a major cause of relationship breakdown, the betrayal of trust often proving more devastating than the debt itself. If we're in financial difficulties due to losing a job, we may also have to cope with a sense of personal failure or guilt. We may become isolated, withdrawn and depressed.

Life after debt

However bad the problem, however trapped you or a loved one or friend might feel, it's important to know that there's always hope. When the widow cries out to Elisha, she takes the first and most important step in tackling debt: talking about it. It can be very hard to admit to *ourselves* that we have a problem. We've known people to wait up to a year or more before seeking help, and even then it's often been a crisis, such as a court summons, that's precipitated action. It's also hard to admit a problem to *someone else*. You may fear that they'll think you ignorant or foolish or careless, or that you'll lose face. Hopefully, however, you'll find that facing up to the truth is liberating. God longs for us all to be free from the burden of debt; with his help we can develop a way of thinking about and managing money that will lead to true financial freedom. Let's look now at some practical steps you can take if you're deeply in debt.

Practical help – preparing a debt-repayment schedule

Your goal is to repay all your creditors, the people to whom you owe money, so far as it lies in your power to do so. This will involve making a list of

Web article

Debt Freedom Day:
Breaking free of debt

everything you owe, and using any surplus in your budget to make regular payments – this is a 'debt-repayment schedule'. (If you feel that you just don't have the energy or understanding to tackle such a task, but you are struggling to pay your debts, don't despair. The debt charities listed in the Useful Addresses section at the end of this book will give free, confidential and impartial advice, and help you complete what's called a Debt Management Plan,[7] if that's the right move for you.)

As a general guide, pay your *priority debts* first – those where the consequences of *not* paying would be most serious. Your credit card debt may be uncomfortably large – but you could lose your home if you don't keep up with your mortgage; face prison if you deliberately avoid Council Tax or Inland Revenue payments; be cut off if you don't pay your gas or electricity bills.

In Chapter 2, on budgeting, we said that your budget should include at least the minimum payments on any outstanding debts. When we discussed assets and liabilities, we showed you how to list, in an assets and liabilities statement, all the cash and things of value that you have (assets), and all your debts (liabilities). Table 4.1 (overleaf) shows in greater detail how the Spender family's debts have been recorded.

Beside each debt, the Spenders have listed the minimum payments they must make. They've also included missed payments and the amount they're behind (their arrears). The total monthly repayments, balance due and outstanding arrears figures appear along the bottom of the table.

Let's assume the Spenders have a surplus of £125 a month to pay off their debts. First, they must address their priorities:

Table 4.1 Debt list

Name: The Spender family

Date: 1 January 2009

Creditor	Item purchased	Monthly payment (£)	Balance due (£)	Pay-off date	Interest (%)	Payments outstanding	Amount in arrears (£)
Store	TV	20	400	None	29	Nil	
Credit card	Furniture	30	600	None	19	Nil	
Credit card	Various	20	500	None	21	Nil	
Speedy's	Car	150	5,000	12/2013	20	3	450
Happy Bank	Extension	100	2,000	12/2012	7.9	3	300
Overdraft	No idea!	50	600	None	10	Nil	
Family	Holiday	?	1,200	No date	Nil	Nil	
Subtotal		*370*	*10,300*				*750*
Priorities							
Mortgage	House	330	30,000	2019	7	3	990
Council	Council Tax	120	700	02/2010		1	120
Total debts		*820*	*41,000*				*1,860*

Dealing with debt

mortgage and Council Tax. They're £990 in arrears on their
mortgage, so if they increase payments by £90, the arrears
will be paid off within one year. An additional £15 a month
will pay off their Council Tax arrears in eight months. Next,
the Spender family look to reduce their non-priority debts.
They talk to Speedy's and the bank, and get agreement to
keep making minimum payments of £10 per calendar month
on their car and house extension loans. They explain that in
a year's time, when they've cleared their mortgage arrears,
they'll be able to catch up very quickly on their debt repayments. Table 4.2 reflects what their debt-repayment schedule
now looks like.

Table 4.2 Reducing-debt list

Debt	Amount outstanding (£)	Extra monthly repayments (£)	Number of additional payments
Mortgage	990	90	11
Council Tax	120	15	8
Extension loan	300	10	Ongoing
Car loan	450	10	Ongoing
Total	1,860	125	

After 11 months, when the priority bills have been paid off
in full, £125 a month becomes available to reduce their arrears
on the car and extension loans. Their revised debt-repayment
schedule, in Table 4.3, shows that their arrears will be paid off
in full after five months.

Table 4.3 Further-reducing-debt list

Debt	Amount outstanding (£)	Extra monthly repayments (£)	Number of additional payments
Extension loan	190	50	4
Car loan	340	75	5
Total	530	125	

61

Snowballing

Now that they have no payment arrears, the Spenders are not *in debt* in the sense of missing payments, but they still *have* debts – they still owe money on other items, and they're paying some high interest rates. They must of course keep up all their current minimum payments, but they can now use their freed-up £125 to clear their remaining debt. A good way to do this is 'snowballing'. Snowballing is using your surplus to focus on one debt and then, when that debt is cleared, adding the amount you no longer need to pay towards it to your original surplus, in order to clear another debt more quickly. For example, the Spenders might first deal with their TV loan (see Table 4.1). It's a small amount but it carries a high rate of interest. They originally owed £400 but have kept to their minimum payments of £20 a month for the 11 months it took to pay off their *priority* debts of mortgage and Council Tax, and the further 5 months they spent paying off the arrears on their car and extension loans. So after 16 payments of £20 they now owe just £80, *plus the interest at 29 per cent*. As soon as they pay off this debt in full in, say, two months, they'll have a surplus of £125 plus an additional £20, making £145.

The Spenders then decide to concentrate on the credit card balance for their furniture. Originally they owed £600, but there have been 16 months of £30 minimum payments during which their mortgage, Council Tax, car and extension arrears were paid off, and two months of £30 while the TV was being paid off. Their balance on the furniture is now £60, *plus interest at 19 per cent*, so after a couple more months they'll have cleared this and released an additional £30 to pay off other debts. They'll then be able to concentrate on clearing all the smaller credit balances or focus on the biggest debt, the car loan.

Snowballing is a useful tool, *but not everyone can do what the Spenders did*. If you're on a Debt Management Plan, all your available surplus will be allocated to debts and there may not be anything to play with at all. But if you do find some surplus, snowballing is a good way of making progress. It puts you in charge, and the psychological benefits are huge.

Multiple debt-repayment schedules

You may find it helpful to complete a debt-repayment schedule for each outstanding debt. This is a simple sheet, one for each debt, that lists the amount of each monthly payment, the date it's due, the number of remaining payments and a reducing loan balance that includes interest charges.

How can the church help people with debt problems?

Churches have a presence in every community in the land and are uniquely placed to offer practical, personal support to people struggling with

Web article

How can the church help people in debt?

debt. They can raise awareness in congregations and communities, both of the scale of the debt problem and of local sources of debt advice. They can also provide simple systems of pastoral care – indeed, many churches have now set up debt advice centres.

Challenges

At the end of the last chapter we invited you to take the credit challenge and make an exhaustive list of everything you owe on credit cards, loans, borrowing from family, credit unions, the lot. Now consider these questions.

- Am I surprised, shocked or fearful at the total amount that I owe?
- Am I only making minimum repayments on any cards?
- Do these debts cause me anxiety, loss of sleep or make me nervous about opening bills?

- Do I have debts on more than three credit cards?
- Am I anxious or embarrassed talking to my partner about these debts?
- Do I feel out of control or out of my depth when it comes to managing money?

If you've answered yes to two or more of these questions, you're certainly suffering from money anxiety. You may well also have a debt problem.

We suggest the following:

- Draw up a debt-repayment schedule, so that you can pay off any arrears and all your credit balance debts as soon as practical.
- Think about approaching a non-judgemental friend who could help by offering a listening ear.
- If things seem beyond your control, seek immediate advice from one of the debt charities listed in the 'Useful addresses' section at the end of this book.

5

Giving

In a beautiful and powerful passage, Paul writes, 'For you know the grace of our Lord Jesus Christ, that though he was rich, yet for your sakes he became poor, so that you

through his poverty might become rich' (2 Cor. 8.9). It's the grace of Christ himself that inspires us to generosity, and this is the basis on which we'll look at the joys – and challenges – of giving in this chapter.

The gift that keeps giving

The UK charity, Send a Cow, helps some of the poorest households and communities on earth to become self-sufficient. When a cow or other animal is gifted, an important condition is attached: *the first female offspring must be given away to someone else.* Families who've received help don't wait until they're financially secure before being generous to others. They don't hold back until all their own needs have been met. They give, as they have received, and make it a priority to do so. This 'gift that keeps on giving' means that families and communities are not passive, dependent recipients of charity, but partners themselves in the fight against hunger and poverty. It's a principle that wonderfully captures the heart of biblical giving.

Biblical characteristics of giving

Giving born of grace can hardly be reluctant or grudging, extracted by guilt or compulsion from unwilling donors. But the truth is that this is an area in which many of us struggle greatly. It might therefore be helpful to look at four biblical characteristics of giving.

Obedient

John 14.15 says, 'If you love me, you will obey what I command.' When we give, we do it in obedience to – and out of love for – God. Paul notes in 2 Corinthians 8.5 that the Macedonian churches 'gave themselves first to the Lord and then to us in keeping with God's will'. Are we willing to acknowledge that all we have is from God? And do we reflect the generous grace he extends to us in the amount we give to resource the ministry of our local church and those ministries we're inspired to support?

Loving

If we say we love God, then giving will naturally follow. That's why Paul regarded the Corinthian church's gift of money as evidence of their love (2 Cor. 8.8). True Christian giving will always be characterized by love, and we cannot detach the gift of money from the gift of ourselves: 'If I give all I possess to the poor . . . but have not love, I gain nothing' (1 Cor. 13.3). In God's economy the attitude is more important than the amount: although they'd been meticulous in their giving, Jesus rebuked the Pharisees because he could see their hearts (Matt. 23.23). We may need to pray for a heart of love in our giving.

> *Giving isn't God's way of raising money. It's God's way of raising people in the likeness of his Son.*

Joyful

When advertising executive Michael Greenberg, otherwise known as 'Gloves Greenberg', died in 1995, his obituary in *The New York Times* told of his care for the down and outs on skid row in New York. Between Thanksgiving and Christmas, for almost 30 years, Greenberg handed out gloves to the needy. He'd deliberately seek out those who wouldn't catch his eye, and ask only for a handshake in return. Key to this fascinating story was his father, a poor man himself, who'd taught Michael when he was a child, 'Don't deprive yourself of the joy of giving'.

In 2 Corinthians 9.7 it says, 'Each man should give what he has decided in his heart to give, not reluctantly or under compulsion, for God loves a cheerful giver.' In fact we're *commanded* to be joyful when we give (Deut. 16.10–11)! Does your giving express joyful gratitude for all you've received and enjoy from God? You may like to consider increasing your giving, from what feels comfortable to what feels slightly sacrificial, trusting that in the giving will come the joy!

Expectant

Paul writes, 'he who supplies seed to the sower and bread for food will also supply and increase your store of seed and will enlarge the harvest of your righteousness' (2 Cor. 9.10). We should give in hope and expectation of God's provision, promise and blessing. But note that these things are related to how we sow (2 Cor. 9.6). If we sow with little money, little trust, little joy or gratitude, then that's how we will reap. So when we review our giving, we should ask ourselves: Do I expect God to provide enough for my needs and for generous giving? Am I confident that spiritual blessings will result from my generosity (2 Cor. 9.11–14)?

> *'A man there was, though some did count him mad,*
> *The more he cast away, the more he had.'*
> *(John Bunyan, 1628–88, from* The Pilgrim's Progress*)*

69

A personal story

A personal story from Keith testifies to these four character-istics of Christian giving.

When he lost his job in the City, Keith received a redundancy cheque from which he set aside a sum of money in obedience to God's prompting. Two years later at a Christian conference, he met a minister from one of the poorest countries in Africa. Keith is passionately concerned about that part of the world and he asked about the problems it was facing. The minister replied that the desert was encroaching on the arable land, and that there had been no rain for four years: the solution was to plant trees to stop the sand funnelling down. Keith asked what the cost of planting the trees would be. It was exactly the sum God had told him to put aside two years earlier. Now Keith admits that his first reaction was, 'Oh no, Lord, not all of it!' But as he offered the money, his heart began to pound, and when the minister returned from making an excited telephone call home, Keith's joy at giving was substantially increased by the news that it had started raining in the minister's town half an hour before! This is a wonderful testimony to God's promise of spiritual blessing as we grow in generosity.

> *To hear from God, give to somebody and then realize that you're an answer to prayer, is terribly exciting.*

How much should we give?

Industrialist and noted philanthropist Andrew Carnegie used to say, 'He who dies rich, dies disgraced'. Though we may not feel it, most of us in this country are rich by global standards, and one day we'll have to account to God for how we've handled the resources he's so generously bestowed on us.

How do we know how, and how much, to give? In 1 Corinthians 16.2, Paul sets out some practical principles: 'On the first day of every week, each one of you should set aside a sum of money in keeping with his income . . .'

- **Priority** ('On the first day'): How far is giving a priority in your household budget? How much is it a spiritual priority alongside prayer, worship and Bible reading?
- **Planned** ('of every week'): Whether weekly or monthly (or highly variable), we should give according to our pattern of income. Is your giving a regular, planned commitment, tax-efficient where appropriate?
- **Personal** ('each one of you'): Generosity is the hallmark of faithful stewardship for all of us, whether we have much or little. Are you giving personally from what's yours to give?
- **Practical** ('should set aside a sum of money'): If we don't put it aside, we won't have it to give! Are you taking practical steps to prioritize your giving, such as filling a church envelope on payday or benefits day, or setting up standing orders or a charitable giving account?[8]
- **Proportional** ('in keeping with his income'): Are you taking your lifestyle into account when you calculate how much to set aside? Proportional giving is the foundation of generous giving.

Should Christians tithe?

Neither of us has met one person who's not been blessed by *voluntary* tithing (usually understood as giving one tenth of income to the work of the

Web article

Clipping the coin: Reflections on tithing

Church). We've both tithed for many years, and God has proved faithful. But we've met some who've been pushed and cajoled and promised the earth if they do tithe. Then there are those who've concluded that tithing is legalistic (the New Testament is almost silent on the subject), preferring to speak of freewill or Spirit-led giving.

---

*A £50 note and a 50p coin started talking in a bank.
'I go to nice shops, good restaurants and health clubs,' the
£50 note said. 'How about you?'*
   The 50p coin replied, 'I go to church a lot.'

This isn't the place to take sides in the debate.[9] But we do feel
that it's important to offer our thoughts on tithing, understanding that not everyone will agree with them!

- Everyone who's working should seriously consider the challenge to tithe, and not simply dismiss it for either theological or financial reasons.
- A minimum wage is just that. It's not necessarily an adequate wage, and to tithe on a low income is likely to require a change of lifestyle that those on better salaries might not have to make. It's hard to believe that biblical teaching asks more of the poor than of the rich. No one on a low income should feel they're robbing God or being sinful if they cannot tithe.
- Those on benefits, and who've thus not earned any income, should give what they can. That's why the story of the 'widow's mite' is so powerful. Remember that God looks at what we hold back, not at the amount we give.
- If you have problem debts, we advise you to continue giving, even just a little, so that the habit and the discipline of giving isn't lost over time. Once debts are repaid, you can reconsider how much you give as your standard of living improves.
- If you feel challenged to start tithing, but 10 per cent of your income seems too much to start with, decide what sort of percentage you can give cheerfully, and periodically increase this, trusting God for your needs as you go.
- For our giving to be true giving, it needs to be sacrificial or, as Steve (irredeemably Anglican!) would say: sacramental. Many of us should probably consider offering a larger proportion of income than 10 per cent.

> 'I'm afraid biblical charity is more than merely giving away
> that which we can afford to do without.'
> (C. S. Lewis, 1898–1963, English scholar and apologist)

Giving goals

An important way to get to grips with giving is to set goals, just as you would other financial goals. Ask God to guide you into the areas in which he

Web article

Sowing the seed: Where should our giving go?

wants you to give. As a rule of thumb, look to give **locally, nationally** and **internationally.** You may find it helpful to complete a 'giving plan': this will not only let you see your intentions in black and white, it will also provide tremendous encouragement as you see the sums mount up! In the example shown in Table 5.1 (overleaf), a total of £250 is allocated each month. Once the child's holiday is paid for, the spare £25 is reallocated to Tearfund.

Gift Aid

Gift Aid gives you a remarkable opportunity to increase your giving if you pay tax. Churches and charities can provide you with a Gift Aid declaration, while organizations such as Stewardship (see 'Useful addresses', p. 115) can help you maximize the tax effectiveness of your giving.

Wills and legacies

Bereavement is an emotional and highly stressful time, and one of the greatest gifts we can leave our families when we die is a well-organized estate, underpinned by an up-to-date

Web article

Where there's a will: The importance of wills and legacies

Table 5.1 An example giving plan

Date	Monthly giving	Accumulated balance	Local		National		Overseas	Other
			St Martin's	Drugs project	CPAS	Mission	Tearfund	Child holiday sponsorship
01/01/2009	250	250	100	25	25	25	50	25
01/02/2009	250	500	100	25	25	25	50	25
01/03/2009	250	750	100	25	25	25	50	25
01/04/2009	250	1000	100	25	25	25	75	

and comprehensive will. On average it will take less than two hours' planning to arrange distribution of what could well be over 50 years of accumulated wealth and possessions. Yet seven out of ten people do not make a will. We cannot urge you strongly enough to ensure that you do have one, which makes provision for your loved ones and, if appropriate, leaves a legacy to the churches and the ministries you've supported in life.

Conclusion

Giving changes us, creating in us a new perspective on life – in this world and the next. Giving changes other lives too: £20 will feed a child in the Global South for a month, or provide the funds to carry out a simple cataract operation enabling a blind person to see. Most important of all, however, giving glorifies God, whose love for us is exemplified in the greatest sacrifice ever made for humankind – the death of Christ on the cross.

Questions to consider

1 It's often said that Martin Luther commented that everyone needs three conversions: a conversion of the heart, a conversion of the head and a conversion of the wallet. Do you feel you've had your third conversion yet?

2 When did you last seriously review your level of giving to your local church and to the Christian agencies and missions you support?

3 How do you feel about sharing 'your' possessions, a car or home, for example? Are there practical ways in which you could do this more freely?

6

Saving

The subject of saving can make us feel guilty, whether we have little money or plenty. For some, the very idea of saving suggests a lack of faith; we would argue, however, that saving actually demonstrates a humble lack of presumption about the future and about how God will provide for us. Certainly we need to trust in God, but we also have a responsibility to be disciplined in the way we manage our money, and to make sensible decisions and choices. In Jesus' parable, the criticism of the rich fool (Luke 12.13–21) isn't that he created wealth, nor that he stored his produce in his barns, but that he stored *everything* for his own leisure and pleasure. There's a challenge here for each one of us: 'This is how it will be with anyone who stores up things for himself' (v. 21).

Exercising faithful stewardship will not only help build God's kingdom, it will also allow us to provide for ourselves and our families – in the near and long-term future – and to plan joyously for other expenditure. You do not need us to tell you that a high-value item bought with money carefully saved tends to mean a lot more joy than one purchased spontaneously on credit.

Getting started

Can I afford to save?

If you're on a low income, saving may seem almost impossible. However, there are some government initiatives that may help.

The **Child Trust Fund** is a savings and investment account for children. All those born on or after 1 September 2002 receive a £250 voucher to start their account. A further £250 is payable when the child reaches seven, and up to £1,200 can be invested in the account each year, tax free, by family members and friends. The money cannot be accessed until the child reaches 18. Government contributions are due to cease in early 2011.

Another important initiative for lower-income households is the **Saving Gateway**. Starting in 2010, around 8 million people in receipt of certain benefits and Tax Credits will be able to open Gateway accounts at participating Post Offices, credit unions, banks and building societies. For every £1 saved (up to a maximum of £25 a month), the government will add a further 50 pence. Low income families could make an extra £300. At the end of the maximum two-year term, the money can be rolled over into a tax-free savings account called an **Individual Savings Account** (ISA). There are two kinds of ISA: cash ISAs and stocks and shares ISAs. The latter is riskier but offers potentially higher returns. From 6 April 2010, you can deposit up to £5,100 in a cash ISA or up to £10,200 in a stocks and shares ISA each year – a very good option if you pay tax.

How and how much to save

There's no mystery to successful saving: you must consistently spend less than you earn and save the difference! There are few strategies more effective than simply paying a monthly sum into a savings account. What you save in your account will grow as a result of compound interest. Compound interest, which is such a curse when you're in debt, is a real blessing when you're saving. Basically, you earn interest in the current year on the interest you've earned the year before. The amount invested, the interest rate and the length of time you save are key factors.

As for how much to save, we've found 10–10–80 a useful rule of thumb: give 10 per cent of income; save 10 per cent;

live on the remaining 80 per cent. Please don't despair if you find it's simply not possible to save 10 per cent at some stages of life! God knows all our circumstances and appreciates our desire to serve him as best we can.

It might be encouraging at this stage to look at a simple example of how to put money aside for specific items so that they may be bought without going into debt. (We'll then briefly discuss some other kinds of savings.)

In February 2010, Mary and David Brown agreed three priorities for their savings in the next few years: a wedding gift for their son; the celebration of their own silver wedding; replacing their car (see Table 6.1). They already have £1,500 in a savings account, and can save £200 a month. Mary's and David's top priority is their son's wedding gift, so they allocate £1,000 of their existing savings to that. The remaining £500 is split equally between their anniversary holiday and the car.

Mary and David then divide the amount of savings still required by the number of months left before they have to pay for the wedding gift,

Web article

The House of the Wise: Planning your savings?

anniversary holiday and car, to give them a rough idea of how much to save each month. Because the wedding gift is their first priority, they make sure they're saving the £50 they need for this. The special holiday for their silver wedding requires £103 a month, so they save £100, knowing the interest earned will take care of the rest. However, the car requires £115 a month, and they can only save £50 towards it. It's their lowest priority because although Mary uses it to get to work, at a pinch they could make it last another year. They also know that after their wedding anniversary, they'll be able to put an extra £100 a month towards it. And as members of a credit union, if push comes to shove they'll be able to borrow the shortfall at an affordable rate of interest, as long as they repay it within a year.

Table 6.1 Mary's and David's savings between February and July 2010

Annual Savings Plan	2010				
Total savings	1,500				
Monthly savings	200				
Priority	Savings goal	£	Allocated savings (£)	Savings still needed (£)	Months before goal	Required savings (£)
---	---	---	---	---	---	---
1	Wedding gift	2,200	1,000	1,200	24	50
2	Silver wedding	2,000	250	1,750	17	103
3	Replace car	4,400	250	4,150	36	115
	Total	8,600	1,500	7,100		268

Capital savings

The three priorities Mary and David Brown have planned for are one-off capital projects. Are you thinking of changing your kitchen next year, or looking forward to celebrating a child's eighteenth birthday? If so, plan to set money aside to pay for them now. It won't just be there when you want it!

Emergency savings

It's sensible to try to set aside some easily accessible savings – between £300 and £800 is a reasonable guide. If the car fails the MOT, the washing machine breaks down or a new school uniform is needed, you'll have enough money to cope. This means your budget can stay intact and you won't need to load the expense onto a credit card or borrow it from elsewhere. Nearly three-quarters of low-income households say they'd struggle to find £300 in an emergency. Credit unions can really help here, as you can mix and match savings and affordable local borrowing. Is there a credit union near you?

Web article

Credit unions

Contingency savings

If we were suddenly without an income, millions of us would be caught completely unprepared. Benefits provide a safety net, but depending on them alone can be a tremendous shock to the system at a vulnerable time. We should try, *as far as our income and circumstances allow*, to keep around three to six months of expenditure in an accessible account in case the unexpected happens. This money can cushion the blow and give us breathing space to look for another job or adjust to a new situation.

Long-term savings

Long-term savings are often used as retirement income. It's important to know what your pension arrangements are, and how much income you can expect. Should you be thinking of making additional pension contributions? As pension provision is such a complex area, it may well be worth taking independent financial advice.

Ten steps to establishing clear-cut savings goals

1 Seek God's guidance

Pray about where to invest, and if you feel uneasy about a certain area or wonder if it might be unethical, then seek out other possibilities. 'I am the LORD your God, who teaches you to profit, who leads you in the way you should go' (Isa. 48.17, NASB).

2 Decide what you're saving for

It's sensible to have a purpose for your savings. Decide on your goals and then work out how you'll achieve them. 'For which one of you, when he wants to build a tower, does not first sit down and calculate the cost to see if he has enough to complete it?' (Luke 14.28, NASB).

3 Evaluate risk and return

An important factor in saving and investing is the risk/return ratio. The higher the rate of return, the higher the degree of risk there's likely to be. If you're nearing retirement age it's going to be tricky to replace any money lost; if you're at an earlier stage in life you can probably afford to be a little less cautious. But keep in mind the Living Bible translation of Ecclesiastes 5.13–15: 'Savings are put into risky investments that turn sour and soon there's nothing left to pass on to one's son. The man who speculates is soon back where he began – with nothing.'

4 Be patient

Get-rich-quick schemes are definitely best avoided. Usually greed and speed go hand in hand, whereas 'Steady plodding brings prosperity' (Prov. 21.5, LB). Over time your money will work for you, if you're patient.

5 Diversify

You only have to look at events in the finance industry in recent years to know that even major, respectable institutions can crumble overnight. Don't put all your eggs in one basket! 'Give portions to seven, yes to eight, for you do not know what disaster may come upon the land' (Eccles. 11.2). Diversify to minimize the risks, and review what's happening to your investments regularly. If you feel out of your depth, consult a financial advisor.

6 Follow long-term trends

Always invest with an eye to long-range economic trends, and a particularly watchful eye on inflation levels. In a non-inflationary economy, bank and building society accounts will provide an adequate return, but when prices are rising each year, it's better to have index-linked savings.[10] Then the interest you receive will be calculated according to the level of inflation. 'Any enterprise is built by wise planning, becomes strong through common sense, and profits wonderfully by keeping abreast of the facts' (Prov. 24.3–4, LB).

7 Seek advice about timing

Seek godly advice as to the timing of your investment. 'There is an appointed time for everything. And there is a time for every event under heaven' (Eccles. 3.1, NASB). The right investment at the wrong time is the wrong investment.

8 Know where to sell

Before you buy, shop around, take advice and work out where you can sell your investment – particularly if it's something collectable, such as stamps or coins. Never trust the salesman who says, 'If you ever want to sell, we'll buy it back.' In hard economic conditions even selling your house isn't easy!

9 Involve members of your family

All partners, and children old enough to understand, should learn the principles of sound saving. If you're widowed you may need to learn how to manage the family finances and where to go for help if you need it. Older children may have to cope financially if both parents die together. At least leave written instructions on the best way of managing your assets, and work out the implications of Inheritance Tax.

10 Count the cost

Investments can be costly in terms of time, effort and emotion expended. Weigh up everything you'll need to put in to achieve the return you're looking for, and work out if you still want to proceed.

Insurance

Trusting God doesn't mean we shouldn't have any insurance policies, any more than it means we shouldn't save. Steve knows from experience how life insurance can help protect against financial worry and uncertainty at a time of devastating loss. It's also sensible to insure against financial disaster by having house and contents insurance. Of course, we're legally required to have car insurance.

Questions to consider

1 How does my personal money story influence my attitudes to saving?

2 Am I a saver, a hoarder or a spender? What about my partner?

3 Am I balancing my saving and giving?

4 If someone asked, could I explain my saving goals or am I saving with no particular purpose?

7

Helping children to manage money

A friend's son was just 17 when he received a letter from a credit-collection agency. He'd joined the local gym, where the young receptionist, who knew as little as he did, took his child's bank-account cash card and set up a direct debit (which, of course, was never honoured). The result for the young man was a rather harsh introduction to the real world.

A survey of over 1,000 young people between 14 and 18 found that half had already been in debt. Nearly a quarter thought that if they had a bank overdraft they could spend more than they earned each month; one in five that getting a credit card would allow them to buy things they couldn't otherwise afford; one in 20 that there was no need to pay back credit card debt at all.

How can we help our children learn to deal adequately with money? Well, we can talk about it as naturally as possible. We can explain when they come shopping with us how we choose the things we do, and why these – rarely – include the latest heavily hyped wonder product. We can demonstrate putting money aside in order to keep to our budget. We can let them see us recycle materials, save energy and reduce costs in the home where possible. The following sections outline some more practical ideas.

Income

We feel that it's a good idea to give children a small sum of pocket money to manage as soon as they start junior school.

The amount isn't important; what matters is giving them the responsibility of freedom of choice in their spending. They'll no doubt make mistakes (you did!), but do try to let things take their natural course. If the whole lot gets spent on the first day *don't* come to the rescue – mistakes will be the best teacher in the long run.

Budgeting

When you start giving your children pocket money, also try teaching them how to budget. You could begin with three small boxes labelled 'Give', 'Save', 'Spend'. Even a very young child can understand this method, because when the Spend box is empty there's nothing left to buy sweets with! As children get older they'll often be given money on their birthday or at Christmas. Let them feel they can talk to you about what they'd like to do with this.

As they mature, children should participate in every aspect of the family budget. At first your child may think that the family has so much income it would be almost impossible to spend it all, but when the cost of housing, motoring and food are fully appreciated you may experience a rapid softening of position!

Following his redundancy, a friend and his wife put a fairly small amount of money in a box for holidays. They cut a hole in the top of the box and the whole family posted ideas on how the money should be spent. Although there was far less money available than usual, everyone had a say in the final decisions – and a great time!

During the early teenage years, encourage your children to draw up their own personal budget. You might ask them to explain how last week's money was spent before you hand over next week's. You can also advise them on the dangers of advertising and impulse spending, and help them differentiate between needs and wants.

Giving

For young children, the idea of regular planned giving – such as to church – can be difficult, so it's a good idea to encourage them to respond to a *tangible* need, like child sponsorship or Comic Relief. Never be embarrassed to tell your children what, where and why you give – assuming you've got your own giving sorted out.

Saving

You might like to encourage your children to open bank accounts and deposit savings in them regularly, which will help them learn about bank statements, interest and how to use a cash card. (Note that understanding the benefits of compound interest can greatly encourage a child to become a habitual saver.) Support their efforts to save short term for something like a toy, but also long term – perhaps towards a car for later on. Perhaps not surprisingly, some children are more motivated to save if it's agreed that their parents add a corresponding amount on their behalf, though whether to do so can only be a decision for the household concerned.

Debt

It's vital to teach children how easy it is to get into debt, and how hard to get out of it. As we noted in Chapter 6, compound interest works both ways: the 2 per cent interest payable when you're in credit could become 20 per cent or more when you're in debt.

Learning the value of work

There are more and more opportunities for children to spend money, and if they simply receive it as an allowance they'll never learn the importance of working – and waiting – for what they want. Developing a healthy attitude towards work and the financial rewards it brings is also likely to improve children's future prospects of employment in the competitive adult world. The following are some suggested areas of training.

Learning routine responsibilities

You don't become managing director overnight! Children can begin to learn the disciplines of work if they're given daily jobs to do around the house, such as laying the table or helping with the washing up. On a weekly basis, they may be responsible for vacuuming their bedroom, doing some ironing or cooking Saturday lunch.

Your own attitude to work

Many children today don't have a real grasp of what their parents actually do to generate income. Take time to explain your job to them, and bear in mind that your attitude towards it – and to work undertaken around the house – is a major modelling influence. After a hard day at the office, coming home tired and grumpy isn't communicating anything very positive!

Earning extra money

If your children need extra money for, say, school trips, why not encourage them to earn something towards it by doing extra work around the house?

Encouraging your children to work for others

Doing a paper round, waiting at tables or baby-sitting can be a useful, character-building part of your children's education. They'll enter an employer/employee relationship for the first time, and learn the effort that's required to earn money.

If you're involved in voluntary work, try to demonstrate that this deserves the same commitment as paid work.

Gifts

In addition to allowances and payment for jobs, you'll no doubt be moved to give your children the occasional spontaneous gift. There's no need to feel guilty about this. Not only is the expression of unconditional love deeply affirming, it also helps your children to learn generosity and freedom around money. You don't want them *only* to be disciplined managers.

Practical help

A simple checklist like the one in Table 7.1 will help you set goals and see how your children are progressing (a blank version may be downloaded from the website). We suggest you review it at least once a year.

Web article
Small acorns:
A children's money
review checklist

Challenges

1 Once a week, for a month, spend more time than usual with each of your children watching *their* choice of TV. Discuss what you've watched together, the messages in the programmes and what they say about lifestyle choices young people have to make.

2 Take older children to a bank or building society to open a bank account. Talk to them about the difference between banks and building societies, different types of account, how to save and what interest is all about. Help them understand their monthly statements.

3 Make it clear to your children that you believe giving something back is important. An event such as Children in Need can create the context for a discussion about what they'd like to give.

Table 7.1 Your children and money checklist

Income

Are your children receiving a regular income? If so, from what source?
Yes; pocket money. Kate has cash in her piggy bank; Michael's money is
paid monthly into his child bank account.

*Are they performing routine jobs around the house in return for that
income?*
Yes.

What must they purchase from their regular income?
Magazines, sweets, games.

What other income do they receive?
Christmas, birthday and, occasionally, holiday money.

Do you have a 'policy' about what they do with those one-off sums?
We encourage them to save 20 per cent and give 10 per cent. We keep the
rest until they decide what they want to buy.

Budgeting

Are the children budgeting? If so, describe briefly how they're doing this.
Yes. Kate always buys a comic and some sweets, and she keeps money for
those things.
Michael buys a games magazine each week and has a budget for his music
downloads. He uses a basic exercise book, with columns for spending,
saving and giving.

Are your children involved in family budget discussions?
Michael participates in discussion about holidays and Christmas. He
knows that we budget for food each week and that we put money aside
for things like the car. We feel Kate is too young for these discussions.

Saving

Do your children have savings accounts?
Michael has a linked savings account at the building society, and transfers
money into it each month. Kate puts her savings into a pottery pig, which
she has to break to get at the money! They save for things, and we
promise to match their savings as a way of encouraging them.

Do they understand what compound interest means?
Michael does – at least he understands that the longer he saves, the more
his money will increase.

How much do they understand about savings?
So far, only that the bank pays them interest on their account. They also
understand that savings are important if you really want something.

Debt

Do your children understand the idea of borrowing money?
Michael understands what a credit card is and how his cash card is different. They've both borrowed money, but not just because they ran out of pocket money.

Have you taught your children the biblical principles of debt?
We always insist on repayment from pocket money to make the point. We only lend if they've already saved up a good amount towards something they want. They're clear about the difference between borrowing money and a gift we give them.

Are they aware of the true cost of credit?
Michael definitely is; he knows that the credit card costs a lot of money unless it's paid off each month. We also make a point of explaining loan adverts when they come on the TV so that he's wise to what lies beneath them.

Giving
Have you taught the principles of giving?
Yes. For both Michael and Kate, giving is something they aim to do with their pocket money.

Describe their giving.
Michael gives £1 to church and Kate 20p, but they also give to other things through school or church.
Michael has a church envelope that he remembers to fill most of the time. Kate puts her weekly giving in another pottery pig, but one she can open so that she has money for church regularly and also some for other things. As a family we sponsor a child overseas, and Michael and Kate will often give something extra towards this, especially at Christmas and on their birthdays and our sponsored child's birthday as well.

Routine responsibilities
What unpaid jobs around the house do the children do?
Clean their rooms and take out the rubbish.

How do you hold them accountable?
We check their rooms weekly.

Your work
Do your children understand the need to earn a living?
Yes. We're encouraging Michael to think about getting a paper round when he turns 14.

How would they describe your job?
Dad builds houses. Mum is a teacher.

Table 7.1 (*continued*)

Could they help you at work in any way?
They're not old enough yet.

Extra money
Are your children able to earn extra money about the house?
Yes. Michael – cutting the grass. Kate – washing up.

Do you ever give one-off gifts?
Yes. We want the children to be spontaneous and joyful around money,
and to appreciate gifts.

Working for others
Do your children do paid jobs for others?
Yes. Michael cuts the neighbour's grass.

Strategy for independence
*What strategy are you using to ensure that your children will be financially
sound when they leave home?*
We're slowly increasing their responsibilities for money management.
Michael will soon be given a clothing amount each month to ease him
into this kind of spending. By their last year at school we expect them to
be responsible for all their needs, except food and shelter.

8

The ethical use of money

One Valentine's Day (sadly not the day before!), Steve went to buy some Fairtrade roses for his wife. Fairtrade brings enormous benefits to local communities in some of the poorest places on earth. However, the air miles involved in flying the roses from Kenya to England were a significant environmental issue. Steve decided to choose social justice over the environment, but his moral and marital dilemma demonstrates the truth that, when it comes to the ethical use of money, there are few clear-cut answers.

Ethical investment

Traditionally, ethical investment has concentrated on *excluding* certain activities, such as gambling, pornography, armaments, alcohol or tobacco. Ethical investment can also positively *include* social investment, for example in wind or solar energy, and involve influencing companies by engaging with senior management and seeking to promote more ethical practices. All in all, there's a wide range of concerns, among which are the following:

- **Social factors:** Levels of workforce pay, working conditions and hours, health and safety, employment of children, education opportunities and equal rights for women.
- **Company standing:** The honesty and integrity of companies, the quality of their management, the good stewardship of human and material resources.

- **Environmental factors:** The record on pollution, nuclear waste, animal testing, recycling waste products, lowering energy consumption and so on.
- **Moral factors:** Avoidance of gambling, pornography, alcohol and so on.

Ethical consumerism

As consumers of the world's resources, we can send an important message to producers and manufacturers by buying and investing – to the best of our knowledge – in an ethical way. To some degree this has to be done by showing disapproval of *bad* practices, but the major emphasis should be on encouraging *good* practices, sound working conditions and responsible environmental stewardship. We really can fight back against the huge power wielded by major companies in their branding and advertising!

Stewardship of the earth's resources

Due to concern about the earth's resources, the issue of stewardship, which is about looking after what's been entrusted to us, is much to the fore. In the past, we naively believed we could extract fossil fuels and chemicals from the earth, alter the whole nature of countries by draining rivers and deforestation and empty our waste products – including nuclear and toxic material – into our seas, without any real concern for the consequences. There are signs that nature's limit is rapidly being reached, and it's not improbable that this century's wars will actually be fought over forests and drinking water.

It's vital that we exercise careful stewardship over our world's finite resources. If we continue as we are, competition for energy, food and water will only increase, which will lead to rich countries further exploiting poor ones as they desperately strive to maintain growth and quality of life.

Unequal world

Inadequate stewardship of the earth has already resulted in great poverty. To see how extreme the situation is, look at Table 8.1, which lists the differences globally between North and South.

Table 8.1 Our world today

North	South
25% of global population	75% of global population
80% of global income	20% of global income
life expectancy 70 years	life expectancy 50 years
nearly all have enough food	20% don't have enough food
uses 88% of natural resources produced	uses 12%
eats 70% of grain produced	eats 30%
eats 80% of protein produced	eats 20%

Source: Christian Aid

Every minute, 30 children under the age of five are dying of malnutrition.

Why do we live in such a divided world when in theory there's enough food for everyone? The answer, in a nutshell, is greed. The answer is self. It begins with me. So what can we do?

Get informed, get involved

Take time to read and think about these issues, to be informed about poverty and environmental matters. A good place to start is the websites of Christian relief charities, such as Tearfund, Christian Aid or World Vision, and of Christian environmental charities, such as A Rocha. These websites contain extensive background information on a range of issues, and provide opportunities to get involved with ongoing campaigns. You could be the person in your church who writes magazine articles or brings resources to the attention of your church leadership.

Live more simply

All of us should be aiming to live a simple lifestyle, not through guilt but because we can appreciate the impact of wasting as little as possible and recycling as much as we can. If we use recycled paper, we save trees, which preserves the forests and thus prevents dust bowls. Dust bowls cause soil erosion, which stops crops growing – a major cause of famine.

Use your power

So many of us feel that there's nothing we can do, when in fact we can do plenty. A few letters to an MP can make them begin to question their position on an issue. The pressure applied by consumers when Shell wanted to dump an old oil rig in the Atlantic Ocean led to a complete reversal of policy. Investigate the working conditions in the factories that produce those cheap clothes we love so much. If you find children are being exploited, write to the company to complain.

Look at how and where you invest your money

At the time of writing, the only major bank in Britain with a policy of ethical investment is the Co-operative Bank. If greater numbers of people insist on investing their savings, pensions or insurance ethically, more banks, buildings societies and companies will be forced to become socially responsible. You may want to take independent financial advice on ethical investment.

Watch what you buy

Many products that we buy without thinking – chocolate bars, for example – are made from raw materials produced and purchased in the Global South. Are we aware what producers are being paid for their cocoa, coffee beans and sugar cane, for example? A great place to start finding out how things might be improved is Traidcraft's website – . Or you might join the fair-trade revolution! Household names such as Starbucks, Virgin Trains, Tate & Lyle and Marks & Spencer are embracing the concept and practice of fair trade. It's not a perfect solution, nor the only one, but it's changing the lives of people in some of the poorest communities in the world. Be active in persuading local supermarkets to offer consumer choice and to stock fairly traded brands, which of course in the UK includes goods bearing the Fairtrade certification logo – more information at <www.fairtrade.org.uk/>.

Develop an interest in a particular Global South country

By doing so you could help influence Christians on a local or even national scale. You could consider giving up a two-week holiday to use your skills working there. Your own life might well be changed! To find out more, ask about short-term service at <www.christianvocations.org>.

Start on your own doorstep

What can you do to help meet the needs in your immediate locality? Are you really aware of what they are?

Challenge

Take a notebook with you on your next trip to the supermarket or town centre. As you shop, ask yourself some ethical questions: How do I know this garment has not been made in a sweat shop by children who deserve to be in school? Has a fair price been paid to the workers who provide this food – in this country and abroad? What are the issues of sustainability around this product? What are the main factors behind my buying decisions today?

You'll need more time than normal for this visit! Stop off for a coffee (made from fairly traded beans, naturally!), and write down your thoughts and feelings. Don't come home feeling guilty. You're doing this exercise to train yourself to ask questions, not to find out all the answers. Learning to think and act ethically takes time.

9

A steward's commitment

In the wonderful film *Field of Dreams*, Ray Kinsella is an Iowa farmer struggling to make a living. Out in his cornfield one day he hears a voice from nowhere saying, 'If you build it, he will come'. For Ray Kinsella, the challenge was to build a baseball field, right in the middle of his corn. It changed his life and the lives of those he loved. Five hundred years before Jesus, the prophet Haggai challenged Israel to build, not a baseball field, but the Temple in Jerusalem. He also promised the people that they would see the glory and know the presence of God as they did so.

Israel was suffering economic hardship. Haggai was asking for time, money and energy to be invested in the Temple when people's own homes were at risk. We can understand why they said *now is not the time* (Hag. 1.2). But in doing so, they shirked the challenge of putting God at the centre of their lives. ' "You expected much, but see, it turned out to be little. What you brought home, I blew away. Why?" declares the Lord Almighty. "Because of my house, which remains a ruin, while each of you is busy with his own house" ' (Hag. 1.9).

It's very easy in today's society to become absorbed by concerns around money and, without meaning to, push God to the margins of our lives. But Jesus warns specifically against this when he tells us to seek first the kingdom of God and to trust that all the other things we need will be taken care of (Matt. 6.33). This is *never* easy. Debt is about more than money. The fear of losing a home does not equate with lacking a roof over our heads. The wonderful thing is that our God knows these deep *emotional* needs as well as our *material* needs. But it remains true that no aspect of life is more important in determining whether we're living in the perfect will of God than how we relate to our wealth and possessions. If God isn't Lord of our finances then he's not Lord of the most personal and important area of our lives.

So how are we to know we're handling money God's way? The answer is by:

- giving regularly and proportionately;
- not being defensive about money;
- enjoying things but never loving the things themselves;
- resisting materialism and never being 'showy';
- always demonstrating the kingdom of God through joyful generosity of giving and lifestyle;
- using God's precious resources to share his love with a needy world.

We pray that this book will help you become financially faithful before God in day-to-day practical matters. This will undoubtedly take time, but don't get discouraged. Stay faithful. We serve a wonderful God.

A final challenge: a steward's commitment to financial freedom

Web article

A steward's commitment

Acknowledging God's ownership of all we have is never easy. But taking this step can help us receive what he's entrusted to us with enjoyment, gratitude and contentment. In closing, we invite you to reflect upon and, if you wish, sign and date the declaration of a steward's commitment to financial freedom on the next page. A copy can be downloaded from the website.

A steward's commitment to financial freedom

I acknowledge God's ultimate ownership of all he's entrusted to me. I release my material possessions to God: my home, my car, my most treasured possessions, my savings (Ps. 24.1).

I acknowledge God as the giver of all, and also that he entrusts his gifts to me as his steward. I receive back with joy and gratitude all I've released to God, and pledge myself to an open, generous sharing of God's goodness to me. Therefore I commit myself:

- to practising generosity and to honouring God with the first fruits of all I have by giving a percentage of my income as an act of worship, gratitude, and to the service of the kingdom of God (Deut. 16.17);
- to careful budgeting by giving time and practising the skills of good money-management as a steward of all God has entrusted to me (Luke 14.28–29);
- to the discipline of saving by working towards setting aside 10 per cent of my take-home pay (Prov. 21.5);
- to working towards a debt-free life, as an expression of my freedom in Christ, by steadily paying off debts (including mortgage debt) and borrowing responsibly (Prov. 22.7);
- to resisting judgementalism and being ever aware of both the needs and the pressures on the poor in my community, in my country and in God's world (Deut. 15.4–11; Prov. 21.13);
- to being a responsible consumer by learning contentment, practising fair and ethical trading and showing integrity in my financial dealings;
- to teaching biblical principles of money to any children I may have;
- to enhancing my work and relational skills by attending to personal development and recognizing that wealth earned creates obligation to sharing and service.

Signed _____

Date _____

Appendix
Redundancy and retirement

———◆•◆———

Redundancy

During the recession of the early 1990s, around 25 per cent of the UK's workforce experienced redundancy. At the start of 2010, 2.45 million people, or

7.8 per cent of the workforce, were unemployed. The situation is likely to remain quite volatile, and if you're worried that your job might be at risk, do check out the Credit Action redundancy guide at <www.creditaction.org.uk>. This gives you clear information on:

- what you're entitled to from your employer;
- what support you can get from the government;
- how to manage your finances;
- how to plan for the future;
- where you can go for help.

Financial planning for retirement

When we're at our most productive, probably between the ages of 30 and 60, it's sensible to save so that we have healthy reserves when our ability to earn declines. Even if retirement is some years away, it's a good exercise to work out what your day-to-day living costs are likely to be when you give up work (even if only at today's prices). This could help you judge whether your pension provision is sufficient – but do also take independent financial advice. The following summary may be helpful.

- **State pension:** Everyone will receive a state pension, albeit at a later and later age! But it's a mistake to assume that the basic state retirement pension (currently £95.25 per week for a single person and £152.30 for a couple) will provide you with a comfortable standard of living. Indeed, you may not even receive the full amount if you haven't paid enough national insurance contributions over the years (in which case, income support may be available). Around one-third of Britons have no other pension provision. Check what you're likely to be entitled to at <www.direct.gov.uk>.
- **Employment pension:** By law your employer should provide an annual update on your pension provision. Nearly all pension plans allow you to take up to 25 per cent of your pension pot in cash, which can be useful on retirement.
- **Death in service:** Many employers have benefits that will be paid out should you die while in service. As part of your future planning, you need to know what this would mean for your dependants.
- **Additional Voluntary Contributions (AVCs):** Any employer who provides an occupational pension must provide an AVC scheme. Employees can pay into this (up to a limit set by the Inland Revenue) to build up extra pension.
- **Stakeholder pension:** This kind of pension is taken out with a private company and is easy to transfer between jobs. All employers who employ more than five people and don't provide an occupational pension, or a group personal pension with at least 3 per cent employer contribution, have to provide access to a stakeholder scheme.
- **Endowments:** These life insurance policies are designed to pay a lump sum on maturity (often at the end of a mortgage term) or when the holder dies, if earlier. In many cases, performance has been appalling. Do seek independent financial

advice if you've been advised that there won't be enough money to pay off your mortgage.

Your financial plans for retirement will naturally have to take into account your personal circumstances. You may also want to put money aside to do something you've always dreamed of, or to fund a calling to fresh service of some sort. The following might stimulate your thoughts:

- What's the big picture? Are you planning to emigrate? Do you want to go to university or Bible college to study? Are you being called to give significant time to charitable work or Christian service? Is it time to downsize to release the cash value of your home?
- What are the likely demands on your time and resources? Will you be involved in childcare? Will you still engage in occasional paid work? Do you have children, close family or friends living abroad you plan to see regularly?
- How would you like to spend your leisure time? Is this an opportunity for travel, to redesign the garden, to follow your home team to away matches, to play golf or simply to enjoy a couple of hours in the morning with a newspaper in a coffee shop?

Useful addresses

Care for the Family
Garth House
Leon Avenue
Cardiff CF15 7RG
Tel.: 029 2081 0800
Website: www.careforthefamily.org.uk

Christian Vocations
c/o Global Connections
Caswell Road
Sydenham Industrial Estate
Leamington Spa CV31 1OF
Tel.: 01926 487755
Website: www.christianvocations.org

Credit Action
6th Floor
Lynton House
7–12 Tavistock Square
London WC1H 9LT
Tel.: 020 7380 3390
Website: www.creditaction.org.uk

Crown Financial Ministries UK
106 Soundwell Road
Staple Hill
Bristol BS16 4RE
Tel.: 0117 909 4784
Website: www.crownuk.org

Jubilee Centre
3 Hooper Street
Cambridge CB1 2NZ
Tel.: 01223 566319
Website: www.jubilee-centre.org

Stewardship
PO Box 99
Loughton
Essex IG10 3QJ
Tel.: 020 8502 5600
Website: www.stewardship.org.uk

Tearfund
100 Church Road
Teddington
Middlesex TW11 8QE
Tel.: 0845 355 8355
Website: www.tearfund.org

Traidcraft plc
Kingsway
Gateshead
Tyne and Wear NE11 0NE
Tel.: 0191 491 0591
Website: www.traidcraft.co.uk

Debt help and advice

Consumer Credit Counselling Service (CCCS)
Tel.: 0800 027 4995
The Consumer Credit Counselling Service. Freephone Monday
to Friday, 8 a.m. to 8 p.m.
Also visit <www.cccs.co.uk> and use their online counselling
facility, Debt Remedy.

Christians Against Poverty
Tel.: 01274 760720
Christian debt advice in local centres. Use the postcode search at
<www.capuk.org>.

Citizens Advice Bureaux
Your library will know your local CAB, or search by your postcode
at <www.citizensadvice.org.uk/cabdir.ihtml>.

Community Money Advice
Tel.: 01743 341929
Christian debt advice in local centres. Use the postcode search at
<www.communitymoneyadvice.com>.

Credit Action
Tel.: 020 7380 3390
A simple, accessible and free practical debt guide, at
<www.creditaction.org.uk>. There's also a money map that lets
you see where you can get local free help for debt problems.

Money Advice Map
Search by your postcode at <www.moneyadvicemap.com/> for
your nearest debt advice centres, including centres run by many of
the agencies listed.

National Debtline
Tel.: 0808 808 4000
National Debtline is part of the Money Advice Trust, a registered
charity.

Notes

———— •••• ————

1 See <http://www.axa.co.uk/media-centre/media-releases/news-story?
id=20091111_1200>.

2 Martha Snell Nicholson, *Her Best for the Master: Selected Poems
of Martha Snell Nicholson*, compiled by F. J. Wiens (Chicago:
Moody Press, 1964).

3 For an easy-to-use, comprehensive online budget tool check out the
Budget Builder from Stewardship at <www.stewardship.org.uk/
budgetbuilder>.

4 The Christian charity, Stewardship, runs intensive Personal Budget
Coaching training days, equipping people with skills and guidance
to assist others in the preparation of a personal or household
budget. For details visit their website at.

5 Credit unions are mutual savings and borrowing societies usually
run by volunteers. They can be based in a workplace or in a local
community. Members save money with the credit union and can
borrow money at affordable rates of interest. Credit unions serve
all income groups but are perhaps especially important in low-
income communities. The number of them in the UK is growing,
and they're offering members more and more sophisticated services. To read more, search for 'credit' on the website, and to find
out if there's a credit union near you, among other things, visit
<www.abcul.coop>. Churches can and do support the develop-
ment of credit unions in their communities.

6 Preaching and study resources on this story are in the Red2Black
section of the Stewardship website.

7 A Debt Management Plan (DMP, a technical term, not to be
confused with the informal 'debt-repayment schedule' we discuss
elsewhere) is a method for paying personal debts (which typically
have got out of control in the sense of payments due taking too
large a portion of income, or even exceeding it) that involves list-
ing all the debts, assessing income and budget, and renegotiating

interest rates and payments with the lenders, based upon evidence that the result will be a higher likelihood of collection by the lenders. Charities such as the Consumer Credit Counselling Service (CCCS) (see 'Useful addresses', p. 115) do this for you for free.

8 For example, a charitable giving account from Stewardship is an excellent, tax-efficient and flexible way to set money aside for God's purposes – see <www.stewardship.org.uk/give>.

9 For a powerful argument in favour of tithing, see R. T. Kendall, *Tithing* (London: Hodder & Stoughton, 1982). For a detailed treatment and a different conclusion, see Stuart Murray, *Beyond Tithing* (Carlisle: Paternoster, 2000).

10 Index-linked savings are directly related to either the retail price index (to protect you from inflation) or to the stock-market indices (to ensure savings match that of the market and do not underperform). National Savings and Investments (NSI) and all major fund managers have such funds.

Further reading

Alcorn, Randy, *Money, Possessions and Eternity* (Wheaton, Ill.: Tyndale House Publishers, 2003).

Blomberg, Craig L., *Neither Poverty Nor Riches: A Biblical Theology of Possessions* (Leicester: InterVarsity Press, 1999).

Lloydbottom, Mark, *Your Money Counts* (Bristol: Crown Financial Ministries, 2008).

Sider, Ronald, *Rich Christians in an Age of Hunger* (Nashville, Tenn.: Thomas Nelson, 2005).

Swinson, Antonia, *Root of All Evil? How to Make Spiritual Values Count* (Edinburgh: Saint Andrew Press, 2003).